PLAY WITH
THE CHAMPIONS

Ron Klinger

B T Batsford : London

First published 2003

© Ron Klinger 2003

The right of Ron Klinger to be identified as Author of this work has been asserted by him in accordance with the Copyright, Designs and Patents Act 1988.

ISBN 0 7134 8880 8

A CIP catalogue record for this book is available from the British Library.

Printed in the U.K. by Creative Print & Design, Ebbw Vale,Wales

for the publishers $\int \partial \mathcal{S} \, \mathcal{Y} \, \mathcal{P}$

B T Batsford
The Chrysalis Building
Bramley Road
London W10 6SP
www.batsford.com

An imprint of **Chrysalis** Books Group plc

Distributed in the United States and Canada by Sterling Publishing Co., 387 Park Avenue South, New York, NY 10016, USA

Editor: Elena Jeronimidis

INTRODUCTION

Would you like to play like an expert? Who among us would not? This book consists of hands which the stars of the bridge world have played at top-level competition. Most of the time they have performed admirably; occasionally they have slipped and so have their halos slightly. When the latter occurs, the deal appears in this book not to point the finger but for its instructive value. Still, it does make us all feel a little better when a top class player does not find the best solution. The difference between such a player and the rest of us is that the expert stumbles far less frequently.

All the deals and problems appeared originally in *Bridge Plus* magazine. The series is ongoing and if you enjoy the material and style of this book, as I trust you will, you can settle back and tackle a new problem each month in *Bridge Plus*.

On each deal you will be asked at various stages what you would bid or play next. Make a concerted effort to come to your own decision before reading further and seeing the recommended action. By adopting this process you will find yourself thinking along the lines that would be going through the mind of the expert. Do it often enough and you may find yourself thinking like an expert before too long.

Ron Klinger, 2003

CONTENTS

A HAPPY ENDING

It is Teams; dealer South. N/S Vulnerable. You are South, holding:

```
♠ K 9 3
♡ Q 8
♦ K 6 4 2
♣ A 8 5 2
```

West	North	East	South
			1NT
Pass	2♦ *	Pass	?
*Transfer to hearts			

What should South do?

Answer: Bid 2♡. There is no option to refuse the transfer.

West	North	East	South
			1NT
Pass	2♦	Pass	2♡
Pass	2♠	Pass	?

What's going on? What should South call?

Answer: North has shown at least five hearts and at least four spades, and the sequence is forcing to game. South should bid 2NT, denying support for either major.

West	North	East	South
			1NT
Pass	2♦	Pass	2♡
Pass	2♠	Pass	2NT
Pass	3♦	Pass	?

What does 3♦ mean? What should South bid?

Answer: North is showing either a 4-5-4-0 or a 4-5-3-1 pattern and is trying to warn you about the club position. With a double stopper in clubs, 3NT would be appropriate but not without any club intermediates at all.

Raising to 4◇ is risky. There is no certainty that partner has four diamonds. You should mark time with 3♡. This cannot be better than honour doubleton as you would have supported hearts earlier with three-card support.

West	North	East	South
			1NT
Pass	2◇	Pass	2♡
Pass	2♠	Pass	2NT
Pass	3◇	Pass	3♡
Pass	3NT	Pass	?

What do you make of 3NT? What do you do?

Answer: North would certainly not revert to 3NT with a 4-5-4-0 and so you can place partner with a 4-5-3-1 pattern. As partner has not shown great enthusiasm for playing in the 5-2 heart fit, you should pass 3NT. Perhaps partner's singleton club will be helpful.

West leads the ♣Q (no surprise there) and this is what you see:

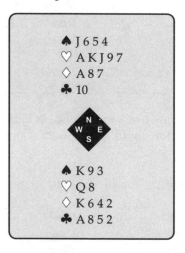

♠ J 6 5 4
♡ A K J 9 7
◇ A 8 7
♣ 10

♠ K 9 3
♡ Q 8
◇ K 6 4 2
♣ A 8 5 2

North's hand is as expected and North was hoping that the ♣10 might add some stuffing to your club holding.

East plays an encouraging ♣7 on West's ♣Q.

What do you do?

Answer: Assuming the hearts are no worse than 4-2, you have eight top tricks. The ninth can come from spades or perhaps a 3-3 diamond break, although you may not be able to give up a trick in diamonds to test that.

The serious danger is the club suit. If they are 4-4, you have only three losers there, but if they are 5-3, you will need to hope that the ♠A is not with the five-card holding. For the moment, there is no benefit in taking the ♣A and so you hold off. West continues with the ♣4 to East's King and you duck again. When East returns the ♣6, you take the ♣A and West follows with the ♣9.

What have you discarded from dummy?

Answer: You can afford to let two spades go.

What next?

Answer: There is no rush to tackle the spades. You may as well run the hearts first and see what the opponents discard. You can afford to pitch one spade and two diamonds.

West follows to two rounds of hearts and then discards a diamond followed by two spades. East follows to four rounds of hearts and then discards the ♣3.

That clarifies the club position, as West must have the ♣J left.

How should you continue? Would it make any difference to you if West had discarded two spades first and finally a diamond?

Answer: There are three basic plans. If you believe that East has the ♠A, you can lead a spade to the King (Plan A). If you believe West began with a 3-2-4-4 pattern and has come down to the bare ♠A, you can duck a spade (Plan B). If you place West with a 4-2-3-4 pattern, you would now cash the ◇A-K, removing West's exit cards, and then throw West on play with a club.

Plan A is almost sure to fail. If East had the ♠A, East would not discard the last club. The complete deal from the semi-finals of the 1998 Vivendi Rosenblum World Open Teams is printed overleaf.

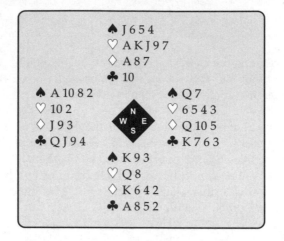

```
                    ♠ J 6 5 4
                    ♡ A K J 9 7
                    ◇ A 8 7
                    ♣ 10
    ♠ A 10 8 2                      ♠ Q 7
    ♡ 10 2           N              ♡ 6 5 4 3
    ◇ J 9 3      W       E          ◇ Q 10 5
    ♣ Q J 9 4        S              ♣ K 7 6 3
                    ♠ K 9 3
                    ♡ Q 8
                    ◇ K 6 4 2
                    ♣ A 8 5 2
```

At all four tables, the contract was 3NT by South. In the first match, at one table West led a spade to give declarer his ninth trick at once. Declarer ducked a diamond and came home with ten tricks, +630.

At the other table, South was Alfredo Versace of Italy. He ducked the clubs to the third round and then ran hearts. West here discarded a diamond and then two spades. This persuaded Versace that West had started with four diamonds and so declarer ducked a spade, playing West for the now bare ace. He thus lost two spades and three clubs, minus 100 and minus 12 IMPs.

In the other semi-final, Bjorn Fallenius of Sweden went for Plan A in the endgame, and led a spade to the king. Minus 100. Curiously, at this table West had discarded a diamond and two spades, while East had also discarded a diamond. Thus declarer could have made three diamond tricks and his contract.

At the other table, South was Marcelo Branco of Brazil. Here West discarded first two spades and then a diamond. Branco read the position perfectly, cashed the ◇ A and the ◇ K and exited with a club. West had to lead from the ♠ A-10 to give declarer a spade trick for +600 and +12 IMPs.

A' HUNTING WE WILL GO

It is Teams. With E/W Vulnerable, dealer North, you as South hold:

♠ 10 9 7
♡ 10 9 2
◇ K 6
♣ A K Q 4 3

Your partner, North, opens with 1◇. East passes.

What should you respond?

Answer: If your bid is 'Two clubs, what's the problem?' you are absolutely right. If you made any other response, you are suffering from problem-syndrome, giving an answer you would not normally give just because you are presented with a problem.

The bidding continues:

West	North	East	South
	1◇	Pass	2♣
Pass	3♣	Pass	?

What do you do now?

Answer: Clearly you are strong enough to look for game, but with a balanced hand and only 12 HCP, 5♣ looks quite a way off. It is better to try for 3NT – but how should you do that? It is silly to up and bid 3NT when partner could have a singleton, or low doubleton, in either major.

Recommended is 3◇, although that is not ideal. Partner will read it as a game try (you would pass 3♣ otherwise) but might pass. In fact partner continues with 3♠.

What now?

Answer: Partner has shown a stopper in spades, but by implication no stopper in hearts. As you also have no stopper in hearts, 3NT ceases to appeal. It is not as though you are likely to receive a favourable lead. After your revealing auction, a passing stranger would lead a heart. Best is to settle for 4♣.

Partner, who has never previously been known to recognise a sign-off, does nothing to disappoint you this time and raises to 5♣. The lead is the ♠3 (fourth highest) and this is what you see:

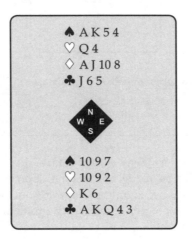

What do you play from dummy?

Answer: Now that dummy is revealed, you wish you were in 3NT. If partner had bid 2NT over 2♣, your 3NT would have been automatic. Perhaps the opposition would not have led a heart, perhaps the hearts are 4-4 or blocked.

Too late to worry about that now. You need to focus on making 5♣. You could duck the opening lead in the hope that West has led from ♠Q-J-x-x, but that is putting all your eggs in one very flimsy basket. If that loses, the opponents are bound to shift to hearts - for where else could they score tricks? No, it is better to take the first trick in dummy, and hope to deal with the spade loser later.

You play the ♠A from dummy and East plays the ♠Q.

What do you make of that?

Play with the Champions

Answer: It looks very much like a singleton queen, and, if so, West has led from ♠ J-x-x-x-x.

What do you play at trick two?

Answer: You would have liked to play hearts early, so that you could ruff your third heart in dummy, but that is no longer practical. If you play a heart and West gains the lead, West can lead another spade. This could result in two heart losers and a ruff for one down.

To escape the threatening spade ruff, you have to draw trumps. When you cash the ♣ J, all follow, but West shows out on the second round of trumps. You play four rounds of trumps in all, and West discards the ♡ 5, then the ♡ 3 (encouraging in hearts), and then the ♠ 6.

You need to do something about your losers in hearts.

How do you plan to eliminate at least one loser in hearts?

Answer: You will have to use the diamonds, and set up one or two extra winners there.

What are the options in diamonds?

Answer: You can play the ◇ K and then lead low to the ◇ J. If West has the ◇ Q, you can discard one heart on the ◇ A. In fact, if West began with the ◇ Q singleton, doubleton, or tripleton, this play will give you two discards on dummy's diamonds.

The other plan is to cash the ◇ K and then lead to the ◇ A, following with the ◇ J, planning to take a ruffing finesse against the ◇ Q with East. As long as East does have the ◇ Q, you will obtain one heart discard, and if the ◇ Q is doubleton, you will have two discards.

Which of these is the better plan?

Answer: If your expectation is that West started with J-x-x-x-x in spades, you will be able to avoid a spade loser by finessing against the jack. Therefore, you need only one discard on the diamonds, and if you score two discards, that is just a bonus.

You should try to deduce which opponent is likely to hold greater length in diamonds. So far West began with one club, and is presumed to have started with five spades. The encouraging discards in hearts indicate at least four cards there – West is unlikely to have discarded down to a singleton heart.

With five spades, four or more hearts, and one club, West has at most three diamonds, and East has at least four.

What is the relevance of knowing the length in diamonds?

Answer: Unless there is very strong evidence to the contrary (based on points held), you should assume that a missing queen or jack is with the player who has greater length in that suit. Your conclusion here is that East has greater length in diamonds, and so you should play East to have the ◊ Q.

Should you tackle the diamonds first, or try the spades first to check whether you are correct in your assumption that West began with J-x-x-x-x in spades?

Answer: You should definitely tackle the diamonds next: ◊ K, diamond to the ace, ◊ J. If East plays low, discard a heart. If East covers the jack, ruff the queen, and then take the spade finesse.

The complete deal from the semi-finals of the 1988 Olympiad Open Teams looked like this:

```
                    ♠ A K 5 4
                    ♡ Q 4
                    ◊ A J 10 8
                    ♣ J 6 5
   ♠ J 8 6 3 2                      ♠ Q
   ♡ A J 8 5 3        N             ♡ K 7 6
   ◊ 4 2          W       E         ◊ Q 9 7 5 3
   ♣ 7                S             ♣ 10 9 8 2
                    ♠ 10 9 7
                    ♡ 10 9 2
                    ◊ K 6
                    ♣ A K Q 4 3
```

In the India *vs* USA match, the USA North opened with a strong 1NT, raised to 3NT by South. East naturally led a diamond, and declarer made twelve tricks for +490.

At the other table, the Indian South, Debashis Roy, landed in 5♣ after the absence of a stopper in hearts left 3NT behind. The play went as described until trumps had been drawn. At that point, declarer tackled the spades before the diamonds.

He led the ♠9, and the USA West could have defeated the contract by covering with the ♠J. That would have removed dummy's entry outside diamonds and declarer would have been unable to return to dummy, even if he had set up a diamond winner there. West, however, played low on the ♠9, and declarer let it run. When that held, South cashed the ◇K, led a diamond to the ace, and took the ruffing finesse in diamonds to land his game, for +400.

That was 3 IMPs to the USA who won the semi-final by 190-126 IMPs, and went on to win the final against Austria by 289-247 IMPs.

THE BIGGER THEY ARE

It is Teams; dealer South; N/S Vulnerable.

♠ A K Q 10
♡ A K Q 2
◇ A
♣ K Q J 10

What should South open with the hand shown?

Answer: With 28 HCP, there is no choice other than 2♣.

What will you rebid after a 2◇ negative?

Answer: Powerful 4-4-4-1s are notoriously difficult to bid. Recommended is a rebid of 2♡, even though partner will take that to be a five-card suit. You are saved that problem since the bidding starts:

West	North	East	South
			2♣
2◇	Dbl		

What does partner's double mean?

Answer: Regular partnerships will have stipulated the meaning of the double in this context. Most popular would be penalties, while others would use it as a take-out manoeuvre, a positive reply denying both length in the opponent's suit and a decent five-card suit.

Your partner's double, however, is used to show a negative reply, 0-7 points. This has become attractive in expert circles.

Why?

Answer: Suppose the bidding starts, in standard style:

West	North	East	South
			2♣
2◇	Pass	Pass	?

South may have a hand short in diamonds and suitable for a take-out double, and most top pairs use double here for that purpose. What if South has a hand suitable for penalising 2◇? It is more likely that opener rather than responder will have such a hand, but if the double is used for take-out, the overcaller escapes the penalty. This naturally encourages many players to overcall friskily.

Having responder double with a negative hand allows opener to pass for penalties and bid naturally with other hand types. Responder's pass can be used for a balanced positive with no stopper in the opponent's suit.

The bidding continues:

West	North	East	South
			2♣
2◇	Dbl	3◇	?

What do you do now?

Answer: As you have opened with 2♣, the situation is forcing to game or a penalty double. In particular, 'Pass' here is forcing – which is a convenient way to handle a hand such as this which has no descriptive bid available. Again partnerships need to agree on method, but it is sensible to have bids as natural, pass as forcing and for take-out, double for penalties. That leaves a bid such as 4◇ to show a two-suiter, preferably both majors (perhaps spades and clubs as well).

The risk of bidding, say, 3♠ with a major two-suiter is that partner raises spades with three-card support when better support for hearts is held. Partner in desperation may even feel obliged to raise spades on a doubleton because other actions are less attractive.

The auction now proceeds:

West	North	East	South
			2♣
2◇	Dbl	3◇	Pass
Pass	4♣	Pass	?

What action do you take?

Answer: As you have a one-loser hand, you can certainly jump to 6♣, but it costs nothing to try 4NT first. If partner has ♣A, it is certainly reasonable to take a shot at the grand slam.

The complete auction is:

West	North	East	South
			2♣
2◇	Dbl	3◇	Pass
Pass	4♣	Pass	4NT
Pass	5♣	Pass	6♣
All Pass			

Not surprisingly, partner does not have the ♣A, but it would be cowardly not to bid the small slam anyway.

The lead is the ◇K and this is what you see:

```
              ♠ 4 3 2
              ♡ 7 5 3
              ◇ J 4 2
              ♣ 9 8 7 4

                    N
                W       E
                    S

              ♠ A K Q 10
              ♡ A K Q 2
              ◇ A
              ♣ K Q J 10
```

You win with the ◇A.

What is the diamond position? What do you play next?

Answer: West will have five or six diamonds, headed by K-Q. East will have three or four diamonds.

You have to start on trumps, so lead the ♣K. East takes the ♣A and returns the ◇3.

Your move?

---

nswer: As West obviously has the ◇ Q, you must ruff this. You ontinue with the ♣ Q to which both follow. Trumps are drawn. West discards the ◇ 9 on the third club.

Now what?

Answer: In spades you have a choice of plays, so should tackle the hearts, where there is no choice. You cash the ♡ A-K; all follow. On the ♡ Q, East discards a diamond.

You can ruff your heart loser in dummy, but you need four spade tricks to make the slam. You could play for spades to be 3-3, or play to finesse the ten.

What is your next move?

Answer: You should cash two top spades before ruffing the heart in dummy. If the ♠J falls singleton or doubleton, your worries are over. On the ♠ A and ♠ K, West plays the ♠ 5 and ♠ 6, and East the ♠ 7 and ♠ 8.

What now?

Answer: The hand is a read-out. Ruff your heart loser in dummy and lead a spade to the ten, knowing that the finesse is a sure thing:

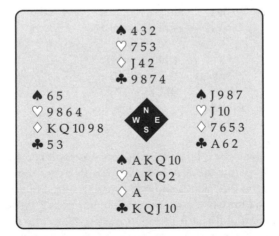

As long as West began with five diamonds the spade position is known. Give West five diamonds, two clubs (known) and four hearts (known), and West cannot hold three spades. After the ♠A and ♠K, West must be out of spades, and the spade finesse is marked.

North did well to bid 4♣. A 3NT bid by North might have been passed and a diamond lead puts paid to that. Similarly, a major-suit bid might have led to an inferior spot as happened on the actual deal from the 1997 USA Trials.

In the match to select the second team to represent the USA in the 1997 Olympiad, both tables reached 6♡:

West	North	East	South
Wolff	Jacobs	Hamman	Katz
			2♣
2♢	Dbl*	3♢	4♢
Pass	4♡	Pass	4NT
Pass	5♣	Pass	6♡
All Pass			

*Artificial, no values

North read 4♢ as a major two-suiter and so bid 4♡, leading to this debacle: East's diamond lead was taken by the Ace, followed by ♡A-K-Q. Next came ♠A-K-Q. West ruffed the third spade and continued with ♢K, ruffed in hand by South. The ♣K was taken with the Ace by East, who cashed ♠J and led a diamond. West had the rest of the tricks. Five down, minus 500.

At the other table:

West	North	East	South
Glubock	Freeman	Lev	Nickell
			2♣
2♢	Dbl*	2NT	3♢
Pass	3NT	Pass	4♢
Pass	4♡	Pass	6♡
All Pass			

*Artificial, no values

Here the lead was the ♡J, taken by the ace. Declarer continued with the ♡K-Q, followed by the ♠A-K-Q. West ruffed the third spade, and knocked out the ♢A. South still had a trump left, and so lost only the ♣A and the ♠J for two down, minus 200, but plus 7 IMPs.

Nick Nickell and Richard Freeman, Bobby Wolff and Bob Hamman, and Jeff Meckstroth and Eric Rodwell, went on to win the match by 252-218 IMPs.

WITH MARKED CARDS

It is Teams; dealer North; E/W Vulnerable. The bidding starts:

West	North	East	South
	Pass	1◇	?

♠ A J 5 3
♡ K 9
◇ A 10 9 5
♣ A Q 10

What should South call with this hand?

Answer: With 18 high-card points, a balanced hand and the opponents' suit stopped, it is reasonable to choose a 1NT overcall. Yet this hand is stronger than just its HCP. There is the second stopper in diamonds, and also the ♣10. While we do not count extra points for these, they are still positive, extra values. In addition, your cards are well placed since most of the missing HCP will be on your right. If partner does not have them, the ♣K and the ♡A are likely to be onside. If so, the ♡K-9 is as good as having the ace and your ♣A-Q is as good as the ♣A-K. All of that should encourage you to boost the value of your hand to 19-20 points rather than 18.

That would make it too strong for a 1NT overcall.

How do you show a balanced hand with 19-20 points?

Answer: After a suit opening by an opponent, all hands of 19 points or more should start with a double. To show a balanced hand with 19 or more points, with the opponent's suit stopped, double first and bid no-trumps next if no better option has presented itself.

You double and the bidding continues:

West	North	East	South
	Pass	1◊	Dbl
Pass	1♡	Pass	?

What should South call next?

Answer: Bid 1NT. This shows 19-21 points, balanced, with the opponent's suit stopped. A jump to 2NT would show 22-23 balanced plus a stopper. If you had doubled with a hand in the 12-15 zone, you would pass partner's minimum reply. A double followed by a bid shows 16+ points. A direct INT overcall shows 16-18 points. Therefore, double followed by a 1NT rebid is stronger than the 1NT overcall and so shows 19-21 points. Had partner responded 2♣, you would rebid 2NT with 19-21 and 3NT with 22+. You just have to take the risk that partner might have nothing. The bidding concludes this way:

West	North	East	South
	Pass	1◊	Dbl
Pass	1♡	Pass	1NT
Pass	3NT	All Pass	

West leads the ♣5 and this is what you see:

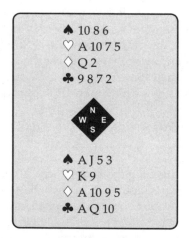

♠ 10 8 6
♡ A 10 7 5
◊ Q 2
♣ 9 8 7 2

♠ A J 5 3
♡ K 9
◊ A 10 9 5
♣ A Q 10

You play the ♣9 from dummy, East plays the ♣4
and you win with the ♣10. Where are the ♠K and the ♠Q?

Play with the Champions

Answer: West has chosen to lead a club rather than a diamond, East's suit. West therefore should have length in clubs, and since East played low, you can place West with four or five clubs headed by the K-J.

You have 18 HCP, dummy has 6 HCP, and you have placed West with 4 HCP. That accounts for 28 HCP, and since East opened the bidding, you can reasonably place virtually every other honour with East. The ♠ K-Q should be with East, who is likely to have also the ◊ K-J and the ♡ Q-J.

How do you continue?

Answer: Once you have placed the cards, it is not hard to set up extra tricks. You can create an extra trick in spades easily enough. At trick two you lead a spade to the ♠ 10 and ♠ Q. East exits with the ♠ 4.

Your move?

Answer: With the ♠ K marked with East, you can score an extra trick by playing the ♠ J. It might work to duck to dummy's ♠ 8 but West might have the ♠ 9.

You play the ♠ J, which wins the trick.

Next?

Answer: East's return of a spade is revealing. A club return would be the natural move, and so you can deduce that East has no more clubs. You therefore cash the ♣ A to see what East discards.

West play the ♣ 3 and East discards the ◊ 3.

What do you play next?

Answer: There is no rush to cash winners. You should set up an extra diamond trick.

Lead the ◊ 10, planning to duck it to East's ◊ J. Later you will run the ◊ Q through East's ◊ K. The full deal is shown overleaf:

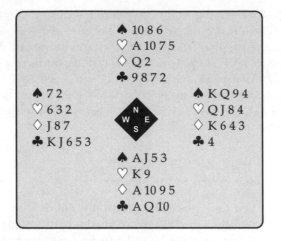

$\spadesuit$ 10 8 6
$\heartsuit$ A 10 7 5
$\diamondsuit$ Q 2
$\clubsuit$ 9 8 7 2

$\spadesuit$ 7 2
$\heartsuit$ 6 3 2
$\diamondsuit$ J 8 7
$\clubsuit$ K J 6 5 3

$\spadesuit$ K Q 9 4
$\heartsuit$ Q J 8 4
$\diamondsuit$ K 6 4 3
$\clubsuit$ 4

$\spadesuit$ A J 5 3
$\heartsuit$ K 9
$\diamondsuit$ A 10 9 5
$\clubsuit$ A Q 10

The hand arose in the 1997 European Open Teams in the match between France and Sweden.

The Swedish South went off after the $\spadesuit$7 lead.

The French South, Alain Levy, played as described, and when the $\diamondsuit$10 fetched the king, declarer had nine tricks.

STAYING IN CONTROL

It is Teams; dealer South; Game All.

West	North	East	South
			Pass
1♠	1NT	Pass	?

What does North's 1NT show?

Answer: 16-18 points, a balanced hand and at least one stopper in spades. A sound 15-count would be enough.

You hold the hand above as South. What action do you take?

Answer: A sensible approach is to use the same methods over a 1NT overcall as after a 1NT opening. If you play transfers, you could bid 2◇ to show at least five hearts. Without transfers, it is more awkward. You do not want to sign off in 2◇ and miss a possible heart fit, and a sign-off in 2♡ is also timid with such good shape. You can try Stayman and if partner has four hearts, you have excellent playing strength.

West	North	East	South
			Pass
1♠	1NT	Pass	2♣
Dbl	Pass	3♣	

What can you deduce about this development?

Answer: West's double of 2♣ shows clubs as a second suit, North's pass denies four hearts and East's 3♣ shows club support.

What do you do now?

Answer: If you pass, it is likely the auction will end now. Partner figures to have three or four clubs, and without heart support there is no reason for partner to bid. It is risky to bid again on your values, but it is also risky to pass. If partner has useful cards in the red suits, you could easily have enough for game. Game would be a good chance opposite as little as:

♠ A x x x ♡ K x x ◇ A K x ♣ Q x x

and partner might be better than that. At IMPs, it is vital to strive for game when vulnerable. It would be contrary to best IMPs strategy to pass when a vulnerable game is conceivable.

How should you continue?

Answer: The five-card heart suit is more important than the diamonds. The auction concludes:

West	North	East	South
			Pass
1♠	1NT	Pass	2♣
Dbl	Pass	3♣	3♡
Pass	4♡	Dbl	All Pass

The opening lead is the ♠ Q and this is what you see:

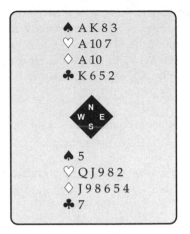

The opponents have an eight-card fit in spades and an eight-card fit in clubs.

What is the spade position?

Answer: The clubs figure to be 4-4 on the bidding. If East held three spades, East would have preferred a 2♠ bid rather than 3♣. Therefore, the spades are probably 6-2.

What is the heart position?

Answer: As East has doubled on what must be a weakish hand, East should have four hearts to the king. You have to pray that East does not hold all five hearts.

What is your first move?

Answer: You take the ♠ A and follow with the ♠ K to discard your club loser.

What next?

Answer: There is no benefit in ruffing either black suit in your hand. With a freakish two-suiter, the best approach usually is to tackle and set up the second suit. You play the ◊ A followed by the ◊ 10. East follows low twice, and West wins the second diamond with the ◊ K. West continues with the ♠ J, which you ruff in hand, as East discards a club.

> *What is your reconstruction of West's hand?*

Answer: Six spades are now proven, four clubs almost certain – and with two diamonds, that leaves West with at most one heart.

> *What next?*

Answer: The ◊ Q is still out, so you lead another diamond. West shows out and you ruff with the ♡ 7, East's ◊ Q dropping.

> *What must you avoid at this point?*

Answer: You cannot afford to lead trumps now via the ♡ A and another heart. East would win with the ♡ K, and both you and East would have two trumps left. When East next leads a club, East will wrest trump control from you. If you duck the club to West's ace, a spade continuation would shorten your trumps again and you could not enjoy your diamond winners.

So far you have lost only one trick (to the ◊ K) and your best move is to ruff a club to hand and ruff a diamond with the ♡ A. That gives you two spades, one diamond, two ruffs in dummy and two ruffs in hand for seven tricks. You have the ♡ Q-J-9 in hand and the ♡ 10 in dummy. If you ruff another club and ruff a diamond with the ♡ 10, you guarantee three more tricks whether or not the ♡ 10 is overruffed.

The deal produced a game swing in the 1996 Open Teams Olympiad quarter-final match between Poland and Chinese Taipei, won by the latter by 132-122 IMPs. The complete deal looked like this:

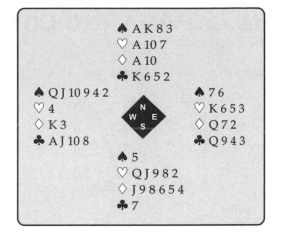

Adam Zmudzinski played 4♡ (undoubled) as described above: ♠Q lead, won by the ♠A; the ♠K for a club pitch; the ◇A; the ◇10 to the king; spade exit, ruffed by South: diamond ruffed with the ♡7; club ruff; diamond ruff with the ♡A. He then led a spade (just as good as a club) to ensure the contract.

At the other table, the play started in similar fashion in 4♡ doubled: ♠Q lead, won by the ♠A; the ♠K for club pitch; the ◇A; ◇10 to the king; spade exit, ruffed by South. The Chinese declarer now slipped by running the ♡Q to East's king (instead of ruffing a diamond in dummy). As we have seen, the bad break in trumps could have been easily anticipated.

East returned a trump won by South who now ruffed the third diamond in dummy. East had two trumps left and so did South, but declarer was stuck in dummy. To reach his hand he was forced to ruff a black card and that reduced his trumps to just one. He now had to go two down for -500 and 15 IMPs to Poland.

THE CAPODANNO COUP

It is Teams; dealer East; N/S Vulnerable. You, South, hold:

♠ J 6
♡ —
◇ A K 6 5 4
♣ A 10 8 4 3 2

The bidding starts:

West	North	East	South
		Pass	1◇
2◇			

You are playing a Strong Club system which prevented you opening with 1♣.

How do you take West's 2◇ bid?

Answer: If unsure about the meaning of an opponent's bid, you can ask the bidder's partner for an explanation at your next turn to bid. If you need to know, do not be reticent about asking.

West's 2◇ is the Michaels cue-bid, showing a weak hand with both majors, usually at least a 5-5 pattern.

The bidding continues:

West	North	East	South
		Pass	1◇
2◇	Dbl		

What does partner's double mean?

Answer: Your partnership can decide how you would like to play Double here. Most top players use Double to indicate a desire for penalties, 10+ points and no great fit for opener, much like the sequence 1◇ - (Double) - Redouble.

The bidding continues:

West	North	East	South
		Pass	1♦
2♦	Dbl	4♡	?

What do you deduce from the 4♡ bid? What action do you take?

Answer: East's 4♡ will be based on four or five trumps and a desire to impede your bidding, with the vulnerability a safety factor for East.

You could pass 4♡ and partner will almost certainly double for penalties.

You would be quite happy with that if your shape were less freakish and if you had a trump to lead. As it is, you may do better by bidding on, but it does not come with guarantees.

You could continue with 5♣ showing both minors.

Is there something better?

Answer: At the table, South bid 4NT to show both minors and imply longer clubs (a result of the Strong Club system).

A 5♣ bid would have implied equal length in the minors or longer diamonds, therefore 4NT for the minors (definitely not Blackwood here) shows longer clubs.

The bidding continues:

West	North	East	South
		Pass	1♦
2♦	Dbl	4♡	4NT
Pass	5♡	Pass	?

What is that 5♡ bid? What do you do?

Answer: Since 5♡ commits you to a small slam, partner's 5♡ shows grand slam interest. No doubt partner has first-round control in both majors.

You have too many gaps in the minors to justify considering a grand slam. In addition, given partner's aim for penalties, you cannot expect a super fit for either of your suits. It is enough to bid 6♣ and let partner choose. The bidding concludes:

West	North	East	South
		Pass	1◇
2◇	Dbl	4♡	4NT
Pass	5♡	Pass	6♣
Pass	6◇	All Pass	

The lead is the ♡2, (the opponents' methods being to lead third and fifth), and this is what you see:

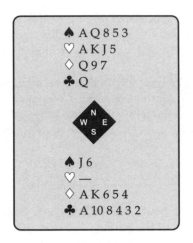

What can you deduce from the ♡2 lead?

Answer: If the ♡2 is West's fifth highest heart, West started with five hearts exactly, and East therefore jumped to 4♡ with only four trumps.

East is unlikely to have done that with a balanced hand and if East has a short suit, it is likely to be spades. With a void in spades, East might have doubled to deflect a heart lead, and so you can reasonably assume that East began with four hearts and one spade, and West with 5-5 in the majors.

Given the bad breaks that are possible on this bidding, you may already be wishing you had left it to partner to double East-West in 4♡. Too late for that.

What do you play from dummy?

Answer: As you may well need all the help possible, you try the ♡J from dummy .

This wins and you discard a spade from hand.

What next?

___

Answer: You will have to do something about all your club losers. The general strategy with a pronounced two-suiter is to establish your second suit. At trick two you cash the ♣A and ruff a club in dummy. All follow.

What does that tell you?

___

Answer: If West began with 5-5 in the majors and at least two clubs, East must have at least four diamonds and so you will have a loser in trumps.

How do you continue?

___

Answer: As it is possible that East has all five missing trumps, you should try to make as many of your little trumps as possible. You cash the ♠A and the ♡A-K, discarding clubs, and ruff a heart in hand.

When you play a third club West follows; you ruff with dummy's ◇9, and East also follows.

What do you know now?

___

Answer: The hand should be an open book. West followed to three clubs and started with a 5-5-0-3 pattern, while East has all five trumps and held 1-4-5-3 originally.

In fact, the complete deal looked as in the diagram on the next page:

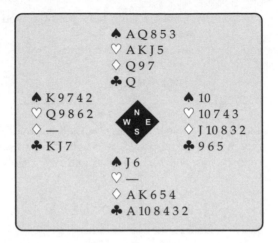

After ruffing two clubs in dummy and a heart in hand, this is the position reached:

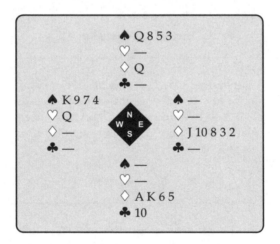

The slam was bid at many tables in the 1992 Women's World Teams Olympiad, but Luciana Capodanno of Italy was the only declarer to overcome the foul trump split. The play went as described to reach the diagrammed ending. A low spade was led from dummy and East was obliged to ruff high. Capodanno overruffed and ruffed her last club with the ♦ Q.

When the next spade was led from dummy, East had no answer. She could make just the one trump trick, whatever she did.

ALL IN GOOD TIME

It is Teams; dealer South; E/W Vulnerable. The bidding starts:

West	North	East	South
			Pass
Pass	1♣		

You and partner are playing Precision.

What does partner's 1♣ opening mean?

Answer: It is artificial and shows 16 points or more, any shape.

West	North	East	South
			Pass
Pass	1♣	1◊	

The 1◊ bid is alerted and explained as showing the 'odd' suits.

What does that mean?

Answer: East is showing a two-suited hand with spades and diamonds, or hearts and clubs. They are called 'odd' because each combination has two suits not only of different rank (major and minor), but also of different colour (black and red).

Many pairs adopt a two-suited defence against strong club openings. With a fit in one of your suits, partner is often able to pre-empt, and so eliminate some of the opponents' bidding space. The strong club works well when given a free run. Rob the opponents of a couple of levels of bidding and it is much tougher for them.

You, South, hold:

♠ J
♡ 10 9 8 7
◇ 7 6 3
♣ 9 8 6 5 2

What action do you take?

Answer: You pass and the bidding proceeds:

West	North	East	South
			Pass
Pass	1♣	1◇	Pass
Pass	Dbl	2♠	?

Partner's double is for take-out.

What do you do now?

Answer: East is now showing spades and diamonds, with spades longer. Since passing the double would show diamonds and spades, and 1♠ was available to show longer spades, East is quite likely to have a freakish hand, maybe 6-5.

You should pass again with this awful collection. Now that East has revealed the suits held, the position is clearer. With a huge hand partner will be able to bid on, with 2NT showing a very strong balanced hand and double still for take-out.

The actual auction took a different path:

West	North	East	South
			Pass
Pass	1♣	1◇	Pass
Pass	Dbl	2♠	3♣
Pass	3NT	Pass	Pass
Dbl	Pass	Pass	4♣
Dbl	Pass	Pass	4♡
Dbl	Rdbl	All Pass	

After South's 3♣, North tried 3NT, passed back to West who doubled. South elected to rescue this to 4♣ and when this was also doubled, ran to 4♡. West doubled once more, and North redoubled to stop South running any further.

The lead is the ♠7 and South awaits the appearance of dummy with more than the usual trepidation. A good partner will abide by the principle 'Put down the good news first in order to reduce your stress level as quickly as possible.' This is what you see:

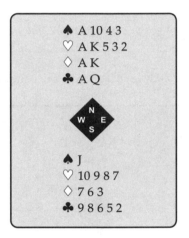

Nothing wrong with your partner's actions.

How do you feel about your prospects?

Answer: If East has no more than six spades, you will be able to ruff one spade. With normal luck, West will not have more than one trump trick and if East is 6-1-5-1, the club finesse is highly likely to succeed.

What do you do next?

Answer: You can afford to ruff a spade. If this is overruffed, you can ruff another spade later, overruffed, and perhaps lose no more than two trump tricks.

You ruff a spade and West follows with the ♠2. It looks as though West started with two spades and East with six.

What now?

Answer: Lead the ♡10 and run it if West plays low. If East wins and returns a spade, you can ruff and if West overruffs, your last trump is high and is the entry to take the club finesse. If West covers the ♡10, win in dummy and if East shows out, ruff another spade. Again, if West overruffs, your last trump is high and you can take the club finesse later.

If West covers the ♡10 and East follows, you can cash another top heart before ruffing the third spade. You then lose at most one trump, one spade and one club.

Is there any reason not to take the club finesse now?

Answer: You'd better believe it! This was the complete deal:

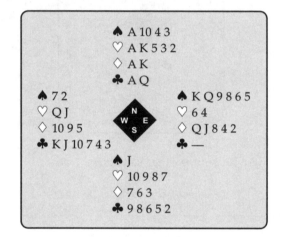

In the quarter-final match between Iceland and Indonesia in the 1996 World Teams Olympiad, the Icelandic South won the opening lead with the ♠A, ruffed a spade, and then led a club to the queen. The defence cross-ruffed tricks three to six for one down. Had declarer played a heart at trick two or at trick three, he could have made twelve tricks.

At the other table, North also opened with a strong 1♣ and East bid 2♠. East later doubled 6♡ for an unusual lead and West duly led a club. East ruffed the ♣Q and declarer could not manage to ruff the three spades without incurring a second ruff. One down.

No doubt the Indonesian North-South were more than a little pleased to learn later that they had picked up 3 IMPs on this board!

THE PIN CUSHION

It is Teams; dealer West; E/W Vulnerable. You are South, holding:

> ♠ A 9 4
> ♡ K Q 10 2
> ◇ Q 8 6 4
> ♣ A Q

The bidding starts:

West	North	East	South
Pass	Pass	1◇	?

What should South call?

Answer: With a balanced hand and the opposition suit stopped, it is best to choose an overcall of 1NT when you have 16-18 points. A double might work out all right, but you could be awkwardly placed later, particularly after a 2♣ reply. If you double and rebid 2NT over partner's 2♣, the expectancy for your hand is 19-21 points.

The bidding ends abruptly:

West	North	East	South
Pass	Pass	1◇	1NT
All Pass			

West leads the ♠ 6 and this is what you see (diagram overleaf):

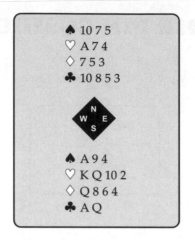

♠ 10 7 5
♡ A 7 4
◇ 7 5 3
♣ 10 8 5 3

N
W E
S

♠ A 9 4
♡ K Q 10 2
◇ Q 8 6 4
♣ A Q

Does anything strike you as odd so far?

_____

Answer: The lead is unusual. The expected lead would be a diamond.

How do you account for the spade lead?

_____

Answer: Maybe West has a singleton diamond, or maybe West has ◇ A-x or ◇ K-x, and is hoping to capture one of your diamond honours.

How many instant winners do you have?

_____

Answer: Five. One spade, three hearts and one club.

Where do you hope to score the extra tricks?

_____

Answer: Perhaps one extra in hearts, and the ♣ K is likely to be onside. You play low from dummy and East plays the ♠ J.

Do you win this or do you duck?

_____

Answer: There is no desperate urgency to gain the lead. Nothing threatens at the moment. As the opponents cannot cash seven tricks quickly, you duck the first spade.

East continues with the ♠Q. You duck again, and West plays the ♠2. East plays the ♠K next, you win this with your ♠A, and West plays the ♠3.

What was the original spade position?

_____

Answer: East has turned up with ♠K-Q-J and West has played the ♠6, then the ♠2, then the ♠3. With ♠6-3-2 only, West would have played either the ♠3, then the ♠6, then the ♠2, or the ♠6, then the ♠3, then the ♠2. The order chosen implies four spades: ♠8-6-3-2.

What do you do now?

_____

Answer: There is still no rush to tackle the hearts or the clubs. If you give up the lead now, the defence can take one more spade and three diamonds at most before you regain the lead.

Why would you want to give up the lead?

_____

Answer: It is worth clarifying the position in diamonds, and perhaps West might lead a club or a heart to you, simplifying your problems there.

At trick four, you lead the ◇4 from hand. West wins with the ◇9, East plays the ◇2. West cashes the ♠8. You discard a club from dummy, East throws the ♡3, and you discard the ◇6. West continues by cashing the ◇A, East playing the ◇10.

What do you now know?

_____

Answer: West began with ◇A-9 and East with ◇K-J-10-2.

West exits with the ♡5 to the ♡4 and the ♡8, and you win with the ♡10. The ♡2 goes to dummy's ace, both opponents following. On the next heart from dummy, East discards the ◇J and West follows with the ♡J on your ♡K.

Now what do you know about East's hand?

Answer: East started with ♠K-Q-J, ♡x-x-x, ◇K-J-10-2, and therefore three clubs. East is down to the ◇K bare and three clubs. The position you have reached looks like this:

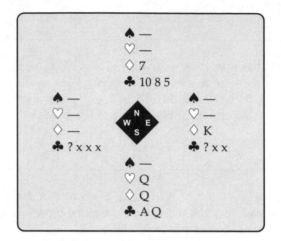

You cash the ♡Q, discarding the ◇7 from dummy. West contributes the ♣7 and, forced to hold on to the ◇K, East throws a club, too – the ♣4.

What are your options?

Answer: If you place the ♣K with East, you can exit with the ◇Q, putting East on lead and finessing the forced club exit.

What if you place the ♣K with West? In that case, you need to hope that East has ♣J-x left. If so, you can play the ♣A, then the ♣Q, pinning the ♣J, and West will have to give dummy the last trick with the ♣10.

Which opponent is likely to have the ♣K?

Answer: This is definitely not clear-cut. East has shown up with 6 HCP in spades and 4 in diamonds. The ♣K would give East 13 HCP, and East might have opened 1NT with that.

However, East was in third seat and 1NT in third seat with 12-14 points is quite risky, especially at unfavourable vulnerability. A suit opening in third seat is often more attractive.

Another slight clue comes from West's choice of lead. West led from 8-6-3-2 in spades when holding J-x-x in hearts and A-9 in diamonds, and therefore four clubs. With four rag clubs, West might equally have led a club as a spade. West did not want to open up the diamonds or the hearts, and similarly may have had an unattractive holding in clubs. Still, that could be J-x-x-x just as much as K-x-x-x. Neither of these ia an appealing lead.

What about West's later play? Here there are two clues. Despite East's discard of the ♡3, West exited with a heart and not a club. If West did not have something to protect in clubs, he might have switched to clubs.

Then there was West's decision to cash the ♢A after cashing the ♠8.

What was that all about?

Answer: West failed to lead ♢A-9 in case that set up a trick for declarer, and yet he cashed the ♢A later, even though this might also help declarer set up a diamond trick.

One plausible explanation is that West was afraid of being thrown in later and forced to lead into declarer's hand. West led a heart next, and so West was not frightened of having to lead a heart to declarer. Therefore West must have been afraid of leading a club. If so, West must have something of value in clubs, and that figures to be the king.

There is no certainty here, but there is a case for placing West with the ♣K. If so, you should continue with the ♣A and the ♣Q.

This was the full deal, which arose in the 1997 European Open Teams in the match between Italy and Spain:

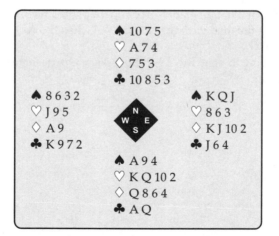

For Italy, Massimo Lanzarotti failed in 1NT after a spade lead. He ducked the first spade, took the second and exited with a third spade.

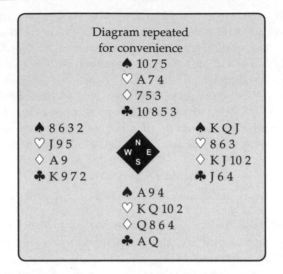

Diagram repeated
for convenience
♠ 10 7 5
♡ A 7 4
◇ 7 5 3
♣ 10 8 5 3

♠ 8 6 3 2   ♠ K Q J
♡ J 9 5   ♡ 8 6 3
◇ A 9   ◇ K J 10 2
♣ K 9 7 2   ♣ J 6 4

♠ A 9 4
♡ K Q 10 2
◇ Q 8 6 4
♣ A Q

East won and switched to the ◇ J to the ◇ 4, the ◇ 9 and the ◇ 3. Next came the ◇ 2 to the ◇ 6, the ◇ A and the ◇ 5. West cashed the thirteenth spade, dummy discarding a club and East a heart.

Declarer discarded the ♣ Q, trying very hard to look like a man who had started with ♣ A-Q-J so that West would not shift to a club. Had West exited with a heart, declarer could win in hand, cross to the ♡ A, and lead a diamond up to his ◇ Q for the seventh trick. However, West did shift to a low club, East played low as well, and now declarer had to cash out to stay just one down.

At the other table, Luis Lanteron of Spain played the hand exactly as described and finished with the elegant ♣ A, then the ♣ Q pinning play to make 1NT.

Italy went on to win the 1997 European Open Teams and Spain finished ninth.

GRATEFUL ACCEPTANCE

It is Teams; dealer North; E/W Vulnerable. You are South, holding:

♠ A K 9 8 7
♡ K 7 6 4 3
◇ A
♣ 10 9

The bidding starts:

West	North	East	South
	Pass	Pass	?

What should South do?

Answer: With a 5-5 pattern, it is standard to start with the higher-ranking suit, regardless of suit quality. (Even with 5-5 in the blacks, 1♠ is the recommended start.) You open 1♠ and the bidding continues:

West	North	East	South
	Pass	Pass	1♠
2◇	2♠	3NT	?

What do you make of East's 3NT bid? What action do you take?

Answer: As East-West are vulnerable, 3NT is a serious bid, expecting to succeed. East figures to have a fit with diamonds plus a stopper in spades, and some outside values as well. If you could be sure of four spade tricks, it would be sensible to defend, but it is not even clear-cut whether you should be leading a spade or a heart.

If partner has a fit in hearts, it could be best to lead a heart, but if partner does have values in hearts, 4♠ should have a good chance. Indeed, if East had passed, a trial bid in hearts would have been sensible. You decide to bid 4♠ partly as a possible save, partly because it might make.

The bidding ends thus:

West	North	East	South
	Pass	Pass	1♠
2◊	2♠	3NT	4♠
Pass	Pass	Dbl	All Pass

The lead is the ◊ Q and this is what you see:

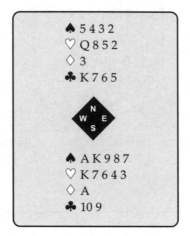

♠ 5 4 3 2
♡ Q 8 5 2
◊ 3
♣ K 7 6 5

♠ A K 9 8 7
♡ K 7 6 4 3
◊ A
♣ 10 9

East plays ◊ 2 and you win with the ace.

What is the diamond position?

_____

Answer: West has length in diamonds, headed by Q-J. That marks East with the ◊ K.

How do you place the missing high cards in the other suits?

_____

Answer: East figures to have ♠ Q-J-10-6, partly because of the 3NT bid, rather than 2NT, and partly because of the final double with only one sure trick outside. Adding the ◊ K to that makes 6 HCP. As East is a passed hand, East can have one of the missing aces but not both. If you are to make this contract, West will have to have the ♣ A and that gives East the ♡ A (without the ♡ A, where is East's 3NT bid?). If East has the ♡ A, the ♣ Q will be with West.

What do you play at trick two?

_____

Answer: You have to lose a heart and a club and so cannot afford two spade losers. You are sure to lose one trump trick and so should play a low spade at trick two. If trumps happen to be 3-1, you are losing the trump trick early. If East has ♠ Q-J-10-6 as you expect, East will win this, and you then may be able to take two finesses against East's remaining trump holding.

You lead the ♠ 9. West discards a diamond and East, after winning with the ♠ 10, switches to the ♣ 8.

What do you make of that?

Answer: The ♣ 8 is the highest spot card in clubs, and so indicates a short suit. Either East has the ♣ 8 singleton or doubleton, or is making a discouraging switch from J-8-x or J-8-x-x.

West takes the ♣ A and continues with the ♣ Q. You play the ♣ K which wins, as East follows with the ♣ 3.

How do you read the club position now?

Answer: West would not continue with the ♣ Q without the ♣ J as well. That means East began with ♣ 8-3 doubleton.

What do you do now?

Answer: Naturally you lead a trump. East plays the ♠ J and you win with the ♠ K. West discards another diamond.

What next?

Answer: You need another entry to dummy to finesse against East's remaining ♠ Q-6. As West appears to have started with ♣ A-Q-J, East is bound to have ♡ A. Therefore you lead ♡ K. If East takes this, ♡ Q will be your entry as long as East has a second heart. If you are to make this hand, the hearts will need to be 2-2.

You play ♡ K to ♡ 9, ♡ 2, and ♡ 10.

What now?

Answer: Naturally you lead a second heart; jack from West, queen, ace. Looking distinctly uncomfortable, East exits with a diamond.

The full deal looks like this:

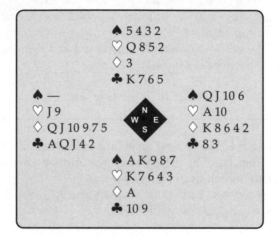

You ruff the diamond exit in dummy, finesse in spades and draw East's trumps and claim your contract.

How would you have managed if West had played the ♣J on East's ♣8 exit?

Answer: You would win with the ♣K and lead a spade. East splits his honours, and you win. Now you exit with a club. Later you play the hearts in the same way, and East cannot avoid giving you a second entry to dummy.

The hand arose in an Australian national teams championship in 1998. The datum (average taken from the scores of the top tables) was +340 to East-West. Making 4♠ doubled is a huge pick-up, but even if you failed you would have scored well at most tables.

As you can see, you would have defeated 3NT comfortably with a heart lead – and even with a low spade lead, you can beat 3NT.

A common result was 5◊ by East-West, often doubled, and almost always making after a spade lead from either North or South.

It takes a heart lead to defeat 5◊, and that is far from obvious or attractive for either defender. Most Wests bid 2NT over 1♠ and East regularly jumped to 5◊ over North's 3♠. Why West chose 2◊ rather than 2NT is not your concern. Just be grateful.

The bidding is as it took place between two of the leading teams.

DOUBLE CHANCE

It is Teams; dealer North; Love All. The auction starts:

West	North	East	South
	2◊		

You and partner are playing the Flannery 2◊ convention.

What does that mean?

Answer: The Flannery 2◊ opening shows a hand too weak to reverse (around 11-15 High Card Points) with at least five hearts and exactly four spades.

West	North	East	South
	2◊	3◊	?

East overcalls with 3◊ and you, South, hold:

♠ A K J 9 7
♡ K J 9
◊ K 6 3
♣ J 8

What action do you take?

Answer: It would be timid to bid only game. Although you cannot hold more than 31 HCP together, the double fit in the majors makes slam possible opposite many openings. Give partner:

♠ Q x x x ♡ A Q x x x ◊ x x ♣ A x

or similar and slam is a strong bet.

What is your bid?

Answer: You might bid 4◇ as a slam invitation, but since you do not need a maximum hand opposite and your main concern is that partner holds at least two aces, Blackwood is best.

The bidding proceeds:

West	North	East	South
	2◇	3◇	4NT
Pass	5♡	Pass	?

Partner has shown two aces and one ace is missing.

What now?

Answer: One does not embark on Blackwood without knowing what to do when the answer arrives.

If you judge that you are worth a slam effort and find an ace is missing, bid six. You can afford one loser. It is just as big a loss to stop in five when six is on, as to bid six and fail.

The bidding does not stop here:

West	North	East	South
	2◇	3◇	4NT
Pass	5♡	Pass	6♠
Pass	Pass	Dbl	?

What does East's double signify?

Answer: It is a Lightner double, warning partner not to lead East's suit but to find an unusual lead.

What lead does East want?

Answer: The Lightner double says 'Do not lead my suit, do not lead an unbid suit.' That means East must want a heart lead.

Why?

Answer: It seems that East is void in hearts and a heart ruff plus the missing ace would spell defeat for 6♠.

Is there any salvation?

Answer: If 6♠ is not on, perhaps 6NT can make. That is what you should bid.

The complete auction is:

West	North	East	South
	2♢	3♢	4NT
Pass	5♡	Pass	6♠
Pass	Pass	Dbl	6NT
All Pass			

West leads the ♢8 and this is what you see:

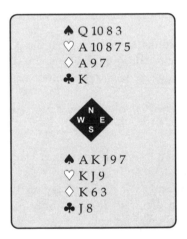

♠ Q 10 8 3
♡ A 10 8 7 5
♢ A 9 7
♣ K

♠ A K J 9 7
♡ K J 9
♢ K 6 3
♣ J 8

There is good news and bad news. The good news is that the opponents did not lead a club. The bad news is that if East is void in hearts as you expect, only four heart tricks are available and you have only eleven tricks on top.

How do you proceed?

Answer: There is little else to do other than run five spades and four hearts.

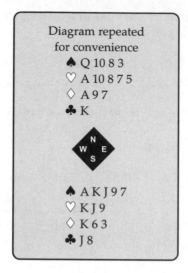

Diagram repeated
for convenience

♠ Q 10 8 3
♡ A 10 8 7 5
◇ A 9 7
♣ K

       N
   W   E
       S

♠ A K J 9 7
♡ K J 9
◇ K 6 3
♣ J 8

Can you see any possibility for a twelfth trick?

Answer: That will account for the first ten tricks. Clearly East is the only one able to guard diamonds and if East also holds the ♣ A and the ♣ Q, you will be able to squeeze East in the minor suits.

What precaution must you take?

Answer: It is important to win the diamond lead in dummy and keep K-x over East.

You win with dummy's ◇ A, East playing the ◇ Q, and run five spades, discarding a diamond from dummy. West follows once and then discards four clubs. East follows three times and discards two diamonds.

You continue with the ♡ K and East shows out, discarding a diamond. You run the ♡ J and follow with the ♡ 9, overtaking with dummy's ♡ 10, East throwing two clubs. You now play the ♡ A.

What do you do if East throws the ◇ 10?

Answer: Discard a club and take ◇ K-6 to make your slam.

And what if East discards the ♣ Q on the ♡ A?

Answer: Now you discard your low diamond and lead the ♣K, setting up your ♣J with the ◊K as entry.

The complete deal is shown below – but don't relax yet! I've got a couple more questions for you:

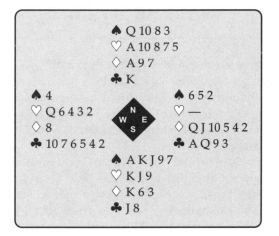

This was the four-card ending:

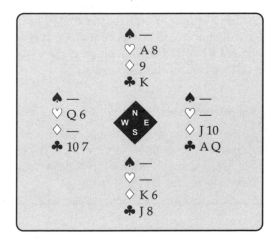

When the ♡A is led, East has no answer.

The deal arose in a qualifying-round match between Iceland and Australia in the 1984 World Teams Olympiad. Bjørn Eysgeinsson played the hand as described to land 6NT. At the other table, after an equivalent start to the auction, the Australian South bid 4♠.

Answer: A club lead would have given the defence the first six tricks.

Why should West have led a club?

Answer: Because East should have continued the good work of his original double by doubling 6NT as well.

Wanting a diamond lead, East would have passed 6♠. When East made a Lightner double, this asked for an unusual lead, clearly a heart on the auction. Given West's length in hearts, it would be clear to West that East had a heart void.

When South ran to 6NT, East would know that South had the diamonds stopped and that a diamond lead would be unlikely to defeat the slam. Passing over 6NT asks partner to make the normal lead, diamonds. Doubling 6NT warns partner off the diamond lead. With East void in hearts and doubling to ward off a diamond lead, the opponents strong in spades, what can East possibly want?

It has to be a club. Suppose North held the ♣Q and East ♣A-K. 6NT still makes on the same line after a diamond lead. It is true that East cannot be sure that a club lead will set the contract but the defence's prospects after a diamond lead are more remote. It is worth investing in a possible loss of 6 IMPs, if 6NT doubled makes, in order to gain a large swag of IMPs when the double works.

Tip: If partner doubles a suit slam to ask for an unusual lead, the double is often based on a void. If the opponents then run to 6NT, partner's double again calls for an unusual lead. Pass asks for the normal lead.

ICE COLD DEFENCE

It is Teams; dealer South; N/S Vulnerable. The bidding starts:

West	North	East	South
			1◊[1]
2♡[2]	Pass	?	

[1] Artificial, 'fert', 0-7 points any shape
[2] Exactly four hearts and longer diamonds

Playing in international teams events, you may come across pairs playing the 'Forcing Pass' in which a pass in first or second seat promises an opening hand (and therefore gives the partnership more bidding space), while most opening bids show 8-12 HCP, thus making constructive bidding by your side more difficult and less frequent. An artificial bid to show the 0-7 point hand is known as a 'fert', short for 'fertilizer'.

Some use 1♠ as the fert at favourable vulnerability, 1♡ at equal and 1♣ or 1◊ at unfavourable. Luckily, you will not often meet these methods in your club games.

It is clearly in your interest to have your defence against such systems well prepared in advance. In this situation, you have elected to have your jump bids to 2♡ or 2♠ over 1◊ show precisely a four-card major with longer diamonds in a constructive hand, 11-15 HCP.

♠ 6 3
♡ J 10 5 4
◊ A 10
♣ A 7 6 5 2

What action do you take as East with this hand?

Answer: This situation is similar to bidding in reply to partner's unusual 2NT or Michaels cue-bid. You have a four-card fit for one of partner's suits, and a high-card-plus-shortage fit with the second suit. Partner is at least 4-5 in the red suits and could be 4-6. If partner has A-K-x-x in hearts and K-x-x-x-x-x in diamonds, you have a good chance to bring in 4♡. You should jump straight to game.

The bidding continues:

West	North	East	South
			1◊
2♡	Pass	4♡	4♠
Pass	Pass	?	

Given that South has at most 7 HCP and is vulnerable against not, this is certainly a surprising development.

What do you make of West's Pass?

Answer: If strong in spades, partner would have doubled 4♠. The pass indicates that partner has nothing beyond what you would expect and is leaving the decision about further action to you.

What do you do now?

Answer: The five-level is usually not the place for a 4-4 fit. The Law of Total Tricks can be of some help here, though its efficacy tends to drop as the bidding level increases. Your side has exactly eight trumps and it seems as though the opponents have ten or eleven spades. If Total Trumps = 19, Total Tricks should be 19. If 4♡ were a good contract, making ten tricks your way means that the opponents should make nine, one down. If you can make 5♡, eleven tricks, they should make only eight, two down. The fact that partner has constructive rather than pre-emptive values should confirm the view to double 4♠. It would be nice to have a trump trick, but your combined strength should be enough.

There is another reason why you should always double in this situation. If you pass, you are giving South a free go at bidding 4♠, a cost-free sacrifice against your game. Even if it costs you 5 IMPs occasionally when they make it, it is worth it to make them think twice about taking a punt in such situations in future. As you should have at least 20 HCP with partner, the double is not fanciful.

Your double ends the bidding. Partner leads the ♡3 (third and fifth leads) and you see (diagram on next page):

Play with the Champions

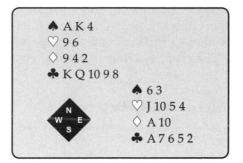

On dummy's ♡ 6, you play the ♡ 10 and South the ♡ 8.

What is the heart position?

Answer: As partner has led the ♡ 3 as the third highest, partner may have a four-card suit including the three and two, but then what are partner's other cards? As declarer did not capture your ten, declarer cannot have ♡ A-K, ♡ A-Q or just the ♡ K. Perhaps declarer has the ♡ A and partner has led from ♡ K-Q-3-2.

Would that be unusual?

Answer: Yes, because in a trump contract it is normal to lead the king from K-Q-x-x rather than risk declarer scoring a cheap trick with A-J doubleton or similar.

What other explanation is possible?

Answer: It is conceivable that partner has led the ♡ 3 from ♡ A-K-Q-3, hoping that you hold the ♡ J.

Why would partner take such a risk or lead low from K-Q-3-2?

Answer: Afraid that declarer may have a singleton heart, partner is anxious for you to gain the lead quickly.

Why?

Answer: If partner wanted a ruff and had a singleton, partner would lead it, but if partner is anxious for a ruff when holding a void, the way to pass that information to you is to make an 'impossible' or abnormal lead, or rather a 'false card' lead in the hope that you can read it as a false card.

What do you play at trick two?

Answer: If partner has a void, clearly it must be in clubs. You should cash the ♣A at trick two and if partner shows out as expected, continue with the ♣2, as a suit-preference signal for a diamond return to score another ruff.

This is the full deal from the 1991 Bermuda Bowl Final between Iceland and Poland:

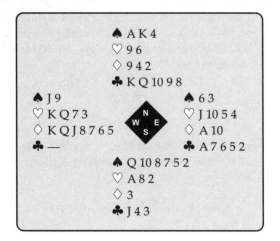

West	North	East	South
			2◇ [1]
3◇ [2]	3♡ [3]	3NT [4]	Pass
5◇	Dbl	All Pass	

[1] Multi
[2] Natural
[3] Pass with hearts, else correct to spades
[4] An out-and-out gamble

This lost the obvious three tricks for minus 100.

At the other table:

West	North	East	South
Baldursson	Zmudzinski	Jorgensen	Balicki
			1◊¹
2♡²	Pass	4♡	4♠
Pass	Pass	Dbl	All Pass

¹ Artificial, 'fert', 0-7 points any shape
² Exactly four hearts and longer diamonds

The play went as described: ♡3 lead to the ♡10, ducked by declarer. Switch to the ♣A followed by the ♣2, ruffed by West. Diamond return, second club ruff, down two, minus 500. That was 12 IMPs to Iceland who went on to win by 415-376 IMPs.

There are a number of features about the bidding and play. First, declarer could have made 4♠ doubled by taking the ♡A and drawing trumps. Clearly declarer was concerned that trumps might be 3-1 and if he drew three rounds of trumps, he would lose two hearts, a diamond and a club. Declarer could not tell the heart position the way that East could, but he might have taken ♡A and played one round of trumps. That holds the loss to one down. No doubt he felt that if he did so, West might win trick three and switch to a singleton club when he had missed this lead initially. If he ducked the first heart, East might find it more difficult to find the club ruff. In practice, East had no such difficulty and declarer paid a heavy price for not drawing trumps.

Second, the deal is not good publicity for the raw count in the Law of Total Tricks. North-South have nine spades, East-West have eight hearts. Total trumps = 17. North-South can make 4♠ and East-West can make 4♡. Total tricks = 20.

One reason is that both sides have a double fit (usually worth an extra trick) and West is void in one of the enemy suits. A void in the enemy suit is usually worth an extra trick.

The World Championship Book described South's bid as 'Balicki's remarkable 4♠ at adverse vulnerability.' As East-West obviously had at least eight hearts and probably nine, Balicki with A-x-x in hearts could easily envisage partner with a singleton, and so North was likely to have length in spades. With no slam-try by the opponents, partner should also have a few points. Not so 'remarkable' as logical.

A MATTER OF SELF-INTEREST

It is Teams; dealer North; Love All. You are South.

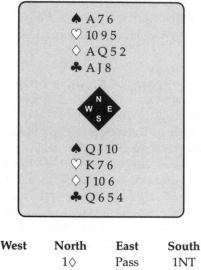

♠ A 7 6
♡ 10 9 5
◇ A Q 5 2
♣ A J 8

♠ Q J 10
♡ K 7 6
◇ J 10 6
♣ Q 6 5 4

West	North	East	South
	1◇	Pass	1NT
Pass	2NT	Pass	3NT
All Pass			

The bidding clearly indicates that partner is not suffering from depression. Will you be able to justify partner's optimism?

West leads the ♡2, fourth highest.

What do you make of that?

_____

Answer: West has no more than four hearts.

East wins with the ♡A and returns the ♡4.

What do you do?

_____

Answer: Since all the finesses go into the East hand, you should hold up the ♡K. If you take the ♡K now, East will still have a heart and you will lose three heart tricks. By ducking, you lose only two hearts.

West wins with the ♡ J and continues with the ♡ Q, East following with the ♡ 3.

What do you play after winning with the ♡ K?

Answer: The suit which will produce most tricks if all goes well is diamonds. You run the ◊ J, West playing the seven and East winning with the king. A diamond is returned, taken by your ten.

What next?

Answer: You have one heart and three diamond tricks. If the ♠ K is onside, the spade finesse, repeated, will bring your tally to seven and you can easily score two club tricks without allowing West to come on lead.

You lead the ♠ Q. West plays the nine, low from dummy and East wins with the king. East returns a spade.

Where should you win that?

Answer: If you win in hand, you have no further entry to your hand and will have to commit yourself to playing the clubs there and then. Rather win the spade exit in dummy, so that you can cash the diamonds and return to your hand in spades. You might gain some valuable information about the opponents' hands by playing off these extra cards.

You win the spade in dummy, West following. When you cash the ◊ A, West discards a club.

What does that tell you?

Answer: West began with just two diamonds. So far, you can place West with four hearts and two diamonds.

You cash your next diamond, discarding a club from hand, and West discards another club. When you play a spade to your hand, West discards the ♡ 8.

What do you know now?

Answer: West began with only two spades. Therefore with two spades, four hearts and two diamonds, West must have started with five clubs. The pattern should be 2-4-2-5.

Why did West choose a heart lead rather than from the longer suit, clubs?

Answer: Because your 1NT response to 1◊ denied a four-card major and denied diamond support, and so you must hold at least four clubs. The club lead was therefore unattractive.

You have made six tricks via two spades, one heart and three diamonds. You therefore need three tricks from the clubs.

How can the clubs be played for three tricks?

Answer: With this club combination, you can play either opponent for a singleton king (cash the ace first) or you can play West for king doubleton (lead low to the jack and then cash the ace), or you can play East for 10-9 doubleton (lead the ♣Q first).

Given the information you have about West's hand pattern, which club play do you choose?

Answer: Since West started with five clubs, East began with a singleton club. East cannot hold 10-9 doubleton and as West has discarded only two clubs, West cannot hold king doubleton. Your only hope is to find East with the ♣K singleton. You cash the ♣A, the king drops from East, and you have nine tricks.

This was the full deal (diagram on next page):

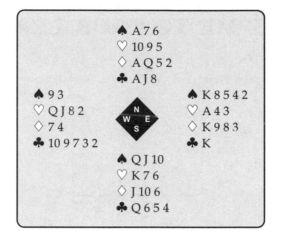

The hand has been modified (minor suits interchanged) to allow for an easier auction. The declarer who played the hand as described was Carol Van Oppen of the Netherlands team in the 1976 World Teams Olympiad.

Suppose that West had discarded a third club and come down to a doubleton. Would your play change?

Answer: Definitely not. As your opponents are strong players, West would not discard so badly to allow you to pick up the whole club suit. There is another compelling reason why you should play East for the ♣ K singleton.

What reason is that?

Answer: If West held the ♣ K, a strong defender in the East seat would have ducked the first spade, taken the second and then locked you in dummy with a third spade. Similarly, East did not have to take the first round of diamonds but could have ducked that, won the second diamond and again locked you in dummy with a third diamond.

Why did East defend as he did, winning the first round of each finesse and returning the suit? Because East was frightened that, stuck in dummy, you would be forced to cash the ♣ A and drop the bare king.

One is rarely wrong if one judges that an opponent is playing or defending in a particular manner out of self-interest.

TAKE ME TO YOUR LEADER

It is Teams; dealer West; Love All. You are West, holding:

♠ J 10 5 4
♡ J 8 7
♢ A J 10 9 6
♣ 4

West	North	East	South
Pass	Pass	1♠	Dbl
?			

What should West do?

Answer: After a take-out double, direct raises are pre-emptive. With the values for a limit raise or better, start with 2NT (artificial and forcing to three-of-opener's-suit). West is too strong for a mere 2♠ and too weak for a limit raise. There are four contenders: 3♠, 4♠, 3♢ as a fit-showing jump, and 4♣ as a splinter bid.

At favourable vulnerability the jump to 4♠ would place greatest pressure on the opponents but at equal vulnerability the losing trick count suggests that, with eight-nine losers, bidding to the three-level is enough. As there is no indication that the partnership has ten trumps, the Law of Total Tricks does not recommend bidding for ten tricks.

The eight-to-nine range of losers relates to the diamond holding. Opposite a singleton or void, a suit headed by A-J-10 is poor but opposite two cards or more, with or without an honour, such a suit should be valuable. This is particularly so here, as South is likely to hold at least one diamond honour on the bidding.

As the focus is on the value of the diamonds, the 3♢ fit-jump is best if that is part of your armoury. If not, then jump to 3♠.

Over 3♢ opener can make an informed decision whether to sign off in 3♠ or 4♠ and whether to push higher if the opponents elect to compete beyond 4♠. Playing fit-jumps over take-out doubles is sensible.

The splinter jump to 4♣ has two strikes against it. Firstly, it commits you to 4♠ when the three-level is high enough, and secondly it gives North an easy double to show club length and strength.

At the table West jumped to 4♠. The bidding continued:

West	North	East	South
Pass	Pass	1♠	Dbl
4♠	4NT		

What does North's 4NT mean?

Answer: In competitive auctions at the four-level, 4NT is not used to ask for aces but shows a hand playable in at least two suits. Rather than guess which suit to bid, a player replying to partner's take-out double after a four-level bid can use 4NT to indicate at least a two-suiter and enlist partner's cooperation. Finding the right game is the top priority.

The auction continues:

West	North	East	South
Pass	Pass	1♠	Dbl
4♠	4NT	Dbl	

What do you understand by East's double?

Answer: The double of 4NT in competitive auctions indicates a desire for penalties. In this auction East's double warns West not to bid 5♠, even though West is unlikely to do so anyway.

In real life, East did not double 4NT and the bidding went as follows:

West	North	East	South
Pass	Pass	1♠	Dbl
4♠	4NT	Pass	5♣
?			

What should West do now?

Answer: Having made a pre-emptive raise, you should not bid again unless partner forces you to do so, or has asked for input by you, or you have unbelievably wild shape. Here 4♠ is already more than you were worth and your distribution is routine, not outlandish. Therefore there is no question about your action now. You must pass.

Is West's pass forcing?

Answer: In many situations when your side has bid to game and the opponents outbid you, a pass in the direct seat is forcing on partner who is expected to double them or to bid higher. The pass by a pre-emptive bidder is not forcing. Partner knows the type of hand you hold and it is up to partner to decide whether to bid higher, pass or double.

West	North	East	South
Pass	Pass	1♠	Dbl
4♠	4NT	Pass	5♣
Pass	Pass	Dbl	Pass
?			

What should West do now?

Answer: Pass. Having made a pre-emptive raise, you should abide by your partner's decision. Partner's double is not asking you to bid 5♠. Partner could have done that.

West	North	East	South
Pass	Pass	1♠	Dbl
4♠	4NT	Pass	5♣
Pass	Pass	Dbl	All Pass

What would you lead as West?

Answer: Partner failed to double 4NT and so you do not expect East to hold a huge hand. This is also confirmed by the opposition's willingness to bid to the five-level. Partner passed 4NT but doubled 5♣.

What do you make of that?

Answer: Partner may have a nasty surprise in clubs for the opponents. In that case it probably does not matter what you lead.

This is not very likely. Why not?

Answer: Without a huge hand, it would be unwise to double 5♣ with just a strong holding in clubs as it may drive the opponents to some other suit, which you may not be able to double. Unless the opponents

---

are sacrificing or you can double any contract they reach, be satisfied to pass and defeat their contract when you have a handy holding in their trump suit.

There is a more likely explanation for partner's pass of 4NT and double of 5♣.

What is it?

Answer: Lead-directing doubles at the six-level are common knowledge. They can also be used at game-level in auctions where a pure penalty double can be ruled out. This would apply to a double by a pre-emptive opener. In this auction the pass of 4NT showed that penalties were not uppermost in East's mind, and so it is sensible to treat the double of 5♣ as lead-directing.

If the double is lead-directing, what message is East trying to send?

Answer: The primary message is, 'Do not lead a spade, our suit.' If a spade lead were wanted, East would pass 5♣. There is also a secondary message, 'Do not lead a trump.' It is almost certain that East is strong in one of the red suits, or is void in one of the red suits.

If East is strong in a red suit, which suit is it?

Answer: Given your values in diamonds, it is likely that partner is strong in hearts.

If East is void in a red suit, which suit is it?

Answer: Given your length in the red suits, it is likely that partner is void in diamonds.

So, which red suit should you lead?

Answer: The good news is that you do not need to guess here. Lead the ◊ A. If partner is void in diamonds, you can give partner a ruff. If not, you can switch to hearts.

This was the full deal, from the final of the Year 2000 Bermuda Bowl and Venice Cup:

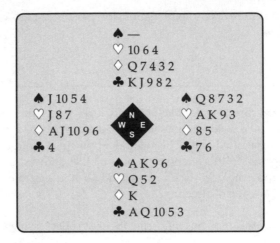

After leading the ◇ A, you do not need to be a member of Mensa to find the heart switch.

In the Venice Cup, the auction went as given except that East passed 5♣. As a result, West led the ♠ J and away went two heart losers. Thus, despite three top losers, 5♣ made for +400.
   At the other table:

West	North	East	South
Pass	Pass	1♠	1NT
3♠	4♣	Pass	5♣
All Pass			

East had no trouble leading a top heart and cashing the second heart. One down.
   As a side-note, East might have opened with 1♡ rather than 1♠ in third seat to show the stronger suit for partner to lead.
   In the Bermuda Bowl, Brazil played in 4♣ by South and made ten tricks for +130 while USA scored +150 in 3♣ by South. At both tables East passed in third seat and South opened 1♣.

SEAMON SEES MORE

It is Teams; dealer West; E/W Vulnerable. You are South, holding:

```
♠ Q 4 2
♡ K
◇ K J 10 6 3
♣ K Q 10 3
```

The bidding starts:

West	North	East	South
Pass	1♡	Pass	2◇
Pass	3◇	Pass	?

What should South bid?

Answer: Partner has shown a minimum opening with five hearts and four diamonds as expectancy. If you head for 5◇, you might lose the first three spades even if partner has three aces and the ◇ Q. If partner does not have three Aces, 5◇ might easily be off three tricks on top.

You have no scientific way of exploring whether 3NT is superior to 5◇ and so you should simply grasp the nettle. Bid 3NT.

West leads the ♠ 10 to East's king, and this is what you see (diagram on next page):

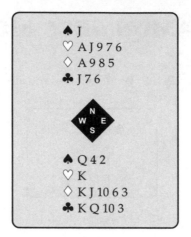

The ♠ 6 is returned.

What do you play on that?

Answer: The sight of dummy has done nothing to persuade you that 3NT is where you wish to be. At least 5◊ would require little more than avoiding a trump loser. No point in worrying about that now, though. Focus on 3NT.

You cannot gain by playing low on East's spade return. Close your eyes, say a little prayer if you will, and rise with the ♠ Q.

When you re-open your eyes, lo and behold, you have won the trick. Assuming you are going to make 3NT, how will you find nine tricks?

From the diamonds and the clubs?

Answer: You certainly cannot afford to play on clubs. That would give the opponents one club and four spade tricks for certain.

All right, if you cannot use the clubs, where will you find nine tricks?

Answer: You already have one spade trick and if the diamonds behave, that gives you six tricks. The top hearts bring you to eight. Clearly the only hope for the ninth trick is from the heart suit.

What position in hearts would enable you to score three tricks there?

Answer: If either opponent has the ♡Q singleton or the ♡Q-x, you have three heart tricks. This is not very likely, but there is no other hope. You cash the ♡K; West plays the ♡8 and East the ♡2.

What do you make of that?

Answer: The play of the eight suggests that West is more likely to hold ♡Q-x than East.

What is the spade layout?

Answer: With three spades, East would have continued with the ♠A at trick two, and would have done the same with five spades, in case South began with ♠Q-x. Therefore the most likely spade layout is five spades headed by the 10-9 with West and ♠A-K-x-x with East.

If the heart position is as you hope, what follows
from the opponents' holding in spades and hearts?

Answer: If West began with five spades and two hearts (seven cards) and East began with four spades and five hearts (nine cards), West is more likely to have length in diamonds. This becomes even more pronounced if West began with only four spades and East with five.

How should you continue?

Answer: It is possible that the diamonds are 2-2 but you have enough evidence to justify playing West to hold the ◇Q.

In the 1999 USA International Team Trials, Mike Seamon backed his judgement by continuing with the ◇K and playing a low diamond to the nine next. When that held, he cashed the ♡A and was duly rewarded when the ♡Q fell. He had made nine tricks without using the clubs.
The full deal is shown overleaf:

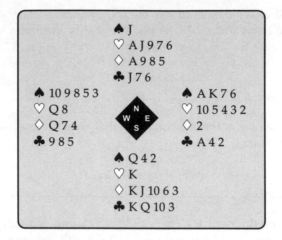

Note that there is no reason why declarer in 5◇ should diagnose the trump position.

THE DEADLY LURE

It is Teams; dealer West; Game All. You are South, with:

```
♠ 9 6 2
♡ 10 8
♢ J 10 5 3 2
♣ 7 6 4
```

The bidding starts:

West	North	East	South
1♠¹	Dbl	2♡²	?

¹ 5-card majors
² Artificial, sound raise to 2♠

What should South do?

Answer: After an intervening bid over partner's take-out double, you are no longer required to bid. The general standard after intervention is:

0-5 points: Pass
6-9 points: Bid at the cheapest level (excluding 2NT)
10-12 points: Jump bid in a suit or bid 2NT
13+ points: Bid game or the opponent's suit to indicate game values

Here your hand is woeful, and so you pass. The bidding continues:

West	North	East	South
1♠	Dbl	2♡	Pass
2♠	Dbl*	3♠	Pass
Pass	Dbl*	Pass	?

*Still for take-out

What do you do now?

Answer: Partner must be very strong to keep on bidding, probably with a 4-4-4-1, or 5-4-4-0 pattern. It is tempting to pass, but cowardice and team harmony persuades you to bid 4♢ which ends the auction.

The lead is the ♠ A and you await dummy with some interest.

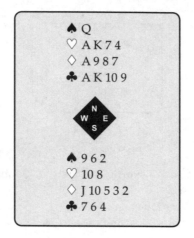

It seems as though you might have done better defending but you cannot worry about that now. Your job is try to make 4♢.

East plays the ♠ 7 on the ace and West plays a second spade, ruffed in dummy (♠ 3 from East).

How do you continue?

Answer: You should start on the trumps, but you cannot afford to play the ♢ A and a second diamond. If an opponent began with ♢ K-Q-x, they could then draw dummy's trumps and cash a spade. You cash the ♢ A and continue with the ♡ A, ♡ K and ruff a heart in hand, East following with the ♡ J on the third round.

You ruff your last spade in dummy, East dropping the king, and exit with a trump, taken by East with the queen, West discarding a spade. These cards remain:

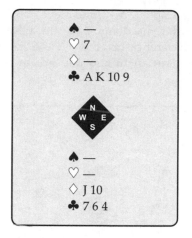

East exits with the ♣2 to the ♣4, the ♣Q and the ♣K. After ruffing a heart to hand (West playing the ♡Q, East discarding the ♣5), you are at the crossroads.

Do you finesse West for the ♣J, or exit with your last trump to East, marked with the ♢K, to force a club lead into the ♣A-10 tenace in dummy?

Decide before reading on.

The deal arose in the 1996 World Open Teams Olympiad in the qualifying-round match between USA and Venezuela:

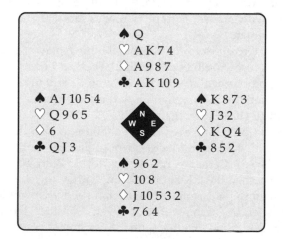

Venezuela's Claudio Caponi, West, and Steve Hamaoui, East, managed to lure the USA South to his doom. After the ♠A and a second spade, ruffed in dummy, declarer cashed the ◇A, the ♡A, the ♡K and ruffed a heart. After a spade ruff in dummy and a diamond exit, the full five-card ending was:

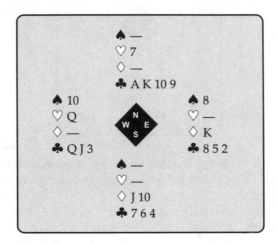

Hamaoui saw that if he cashed the ◇K (West throwing the ♠10) and exited with a spade, West would be squeezed in hearts and clubs, while if he cashed ◇K and then led a club, declarer would be forced into ruffing dummy's heart and finessing West for the other club honour.

Therefore he led a low club at once. Caponi played the queen. Declarer won, ruffed the heart and, expecting East to be down to clubs only, exited with his last trump. Hamaoui faced the ♠8 to put the contract one down.

There were two clues to finding the winning play of repeating the club finesse. North-South began with 21 HCP and East-West with 19. East had already turned up with the ♠K, the ♡J and the ◇K-Q, 9 HCP. As West opened the bidding light, it was more probable that West had started with 10 HCP rather than 9 HCP.

The biggest tip-off, however, is East's failure to cash the ◇K. If East had begun with ♣J-x-x or ♣J-x-x-x, would East have allowed himself to be endplayed? Certainly not at this level. With ♣J-x-x(-x), East would have cashed the ◇K before exiting with a low club.

If you intend to play as the actual declarer did, you would be much better off defending against 3♠ doubled. Consider the full layout again, bearing in mind that this time the declarer is West:

Play with the Champions

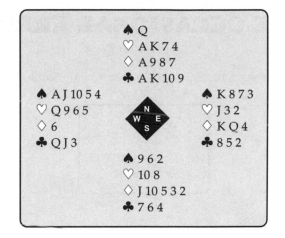

North might well lead the ♡ A (or the ♣ A and switch to the ♡ A after your discouraging signal). Next comes the ♡ K and the ♡ 4 for South to ruff. The club return goes to North. After two clubs tricks and the ◇ A, the contract is already two down.

When North plays a fourth heart, what will declarer do? Declarer has to ruff with the ♠ K to avoid going three down – and there must be a strong chance that declarer will in fact finesse South for the ♠ Q and end up three down after all.

That's +800 or +500! Beats 4◇, doesn't it?

No one said bridge was an easy game.

THE OCCASIONAL ERROR

It is Teams; dealer East; E/W Vulnerable. You are South, holding:

> ♠ 8
> ♡ —
> ◇ A K 10 9 7 6 4
> ♣ J 10 8 6 4

The bidding starts:

West	North	East	South
		Pass	?

What should South do?

Answer: With such powerful diamonds (Suit Quality* of 10) and only five losers, you should open with 5◇ at this vulnerability. While a club contract might be better, it is more important to put maximum pressure on the opponents by a high-level pre-empt. To show a two-suiter is misguided when you have such disparity in length and strength in the suits.

> *What would your answer be if East had opened the bidding with 1♣ (East-West are playing five-card majors and a 15-17 1NT)?*

---

*The Suit Quality (SQ) Test: add the number of cards in a suit to the honours in that suit. Total = Suit Quality. For example:

    A-K-10-9-7-6-4 = 7 cards + 3 honours = SQ 10

    K-Q-J-10-3-2 = 6 cards + 4 honours = SQ 10

    A-Q-J-3-2 = 5 cards + 3 honours = SQ 8

This is a test the author invented to help students judge when a suit is good enough for an overcall or a pre-empt: the SQ should equal or be greater than the number of tricks for which you are bidding when you overcall.

Answer: You are still worth a jump to 5◇ to try to shut West out of the auction. If East has a balanced hand with three or four clubs, you may still be able to create one or two length tricks in clubs, while if East has five or more clubs, that means partner should be short there and so is more likely to have support for your diamonds.

In each case, everyone passes 5◇.

♠ A Q J 3 2
♡ 10 8 5 3 2
◇ 5 2
♣ A

♠ 8
♡ —
◇ A K 10 9 7 6 4
♣ J 10 8 6 4

How would you plan the play:
(a) on the ♡6 lead? (b) on the ◇3 lead to East's ◇Q after East opened 1♣?

Answer (a): You ruff the heart lead and should embark on a cross-ruff. Club to the ace, heart ruff, club ruff, heart ruff, club ruff, heart ruff. Hearts have split 4-4 and clubs 4-3.

What next?

Answer: You may as well tackle trumps for if they split 2-2, you can make twelve tricks either by conceding a club or by discarding a club on the established heart winner. West shows out on the second round of trumps.

What now?

Answer: You can claim eleven tricks safely by simply leading a club, or by crossing to dummy with a spade and leading a major suit through

---

East, thus scoring your remaining ten of trumps en passant.

Any other ideas?

Answer: You are down to a four-card ending:

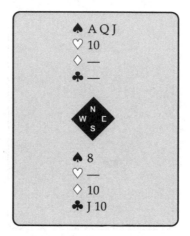

Dummy's last heart is high, East has the last trump, and there is only one club remaining. It is therefore perfectly safe to exit with your last trump. East wins and can cash at most one club. Dummy will then take the last two tricks. If, however, East is down to the top diamond and three spades, you make twelve tricks without risk.

Now go back to the second part of the problem:

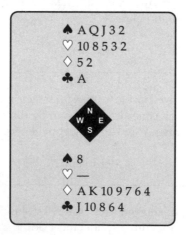

This time East-West play five-card majors and a 15-17 1NT. East opens 1♣, you bid 5◇ and everyone passes. West leads the ◇3 to East's queen.

How do you play?

Answer (b): The ◇3 lead goes to East's queen and your ace. You should ruff one club in dummy, and so the play starts: club to the ace and the ♡2 from dummy, East playing the ace. You ruff this, and ruff a club in dummy. A heart ruff puts you back in hand, West playing the ♡J. You cash the king of trumps and it is no surprise that West shows out, pitching ♡9. East has the ◇J left.

What next?

Answer: There is no point in the spade finesse. Even if it works, you can discard only one club and are still left with two losing clubs. You may as well lead a trump. West discards ♠4, East wins, cashes the ♣K and exits with the ♡4 (West plays the ♡K).

What do you make of that?

Answer: If East held the ♣Q as well, East could have cashed that to defeat you. It is safe then to assume that East started with ♣K-x-x only and you already know East held ◇Q-J-8 originally.

What else can you deduce?

Answer: East must have started with a balanced hand, either 3-4-3-3 or 4-3-3-3. Add the ♡A and East has 10 HCP.

The singleton trump lead by West was very risky and would not have been chosen if a safer lead were available. You have already seen the ♡J and ♡K from West. With hearts headed by the K-Q-J, West would surely have chosen that lead.

You can therefore safely give East the A-Q in hearts. That comes to 12 HCP for East and marks the ♠K with West, else East would have opened 1NT with 15 HCP.

How do you conclude the play?

Answer: With the ♠K and the ♣Q, West can be squeezed in the black suits. Simply play your last trump and if the ♣Q has not appeared, take the spade finesse.

This was the complete deal, which was Board 6 in the semi-finals of the 1998 Rosenblum World Teams Championship:

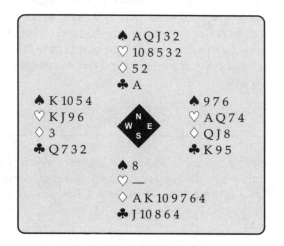

In the Brazil vs Sweden match, after East opened with 1♣, Marcelo Branco of Brazil jumped to 5◊. The play went as described in *Answer (b)* to reach the following ending with one trump to go:

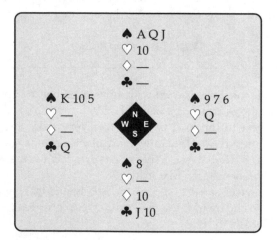

When the last trump was played, West let a spade go, for to throw the ♣Q would make South's clubs high. Branco pitched dummy's heart and took the spade finesse. The ♠A dropped the king and dummy's last spade was high: +400.

How could East have defeated 5◇?

Answer: On lead with the third trump, East can defeat 5◇ by leading a spade, West playing low, or by cashing the ♣K and then switching to a spade. In each case, this removes the entry to dummy and destroys the squeeze. At the vital moment, East knows declarer's trump length and the heart position. If East has received a count signal from West in clubs, East can work out declarer's precise pattern and should be able to find this defence at this level of play.

At the other table, East passed and South opened 5◇, passed out. The ♡6 was led and the play went as described in *Answer (a)*. The four-card ending was:

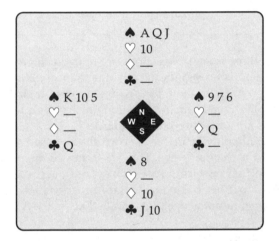

Both the declarer and the report in the world championship book missed the cost-nothing chance for an overtrick by exiting with a trump at trick ten. At the table, declarer led a spade to the ace and so scored the ◇10 for a flat board.

For us mere mortals, it is of some comfort that those who attain the lofty heights can also make the occasional error. The difference is that with us the errors are, alas, not just occasional.

A DANISH DELIGHT

It is Teams; dealer West; Love All. You are South, holding:

```
♠ A J 10 8 7 4 2
♡ 9 6 2
◇ A K 2
♣ —
```

The bidding starts:

West	North	East	South
Pass	Pass	1♣	?

What should South do?

Answer: The three reasonable actions are to overcall 1♠, jump to 4♠, or double. There is no significant advantage in doubling. No matter what partner replies, you will bid spades. To double first and change suit next implies greater high-card strength than you hold (but your playing tricks are adequate compensation).

No one would point the finger of scorn at you for a 1♠ overcall, but the jump to 4♠ is recommended. This places maximum pressure on the opposition. In first or second seat, you would open 1♠, as a slam is possible. After partner has passed, slam prospects are remote when you hold a minimum opening, and that makes the pre-empt acceptable.

When you do pre-empt with a strong hand, make sure that you jump to game. It would be a serious error to bid 3♠ on these cards. To pre-empt to the four level, your Suit Quality should be 10 or more (Suit Quality = Length + Honours in long suit, see page 72) and you should have about eight playing tricks.

West	North	East	South
Pass	Pass	1♣	4♠
All Pass			

When dummy comes down, this is what you see:

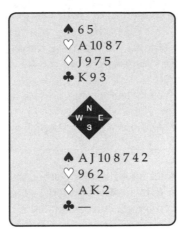

West leads ♡ J.

What do you make of that?

Answer: An honour-card lead normally shows a sequence or a shortage. As the ♡ 10 is visible, West is almost certainly leading top from a doubleton heart.

Why not a singleton heart?

Answer: If West began with a singleton heart, that would give East five hearts. With five hearts, East would normally open with 1♡ rather than 1♣ unless the clubs are longer. It is possible that East started with six or more clubs and five hearts, but it is unlikely.

What do you play at trick one?

Answer: Play low from dummy at trick one. If you take the first heart and West does have the expected doubleton, West can continue hearts later and allow East to cash two heart tricks.

The ♡ J wins and West continues with ♡ 4, taken by the ace.

What next?

Answer: As there is no reason to delay drawing the trumps, you lead a spade from dummy. East plays the king, which you capture with the ace. You continue with the ♠ J, West playing the ♠ Q and East discarding the ♣ 7 (encouraging). West switches to the ♣ J, the ♣ 3 from dummy and the ♣ 4 from East.

You ruff and draw West's last trump, East discarding the ♣ 5.

What do you make of the position so far?

Answer: East has turned up with a singleton spade and four hearts to the K-Q. If East began with a 1-4-4-4 pattern, a 1◊ opening would have been normal in order to have a convenient 2♣ rebid available if East is not strong enough to reverse. That suggests that East started with at least five clubs and might have a 1-4-3-5 or 1-4-2-6 distribution.

The ♣ J switch places East with the ♣ A-Q. That gives East 14 high-card points, and so the location of the ◊ Q is not known.

You are in danger of losing one spade, two hearts and a diamond but if East does hold the ◊ Q, East might well be in some difficulty.

How can you put East under pressure?

Answer: Run trumps and watch East's discards.

This was the complete deal which arose in the 1994 Nordic Championships in Finland:

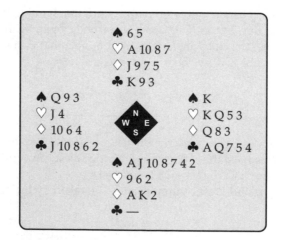

Play with the Champions

After a slightly different auction, Jens Auken of Denmark, South, played as described and continued with two more trumps to reach this end-position:

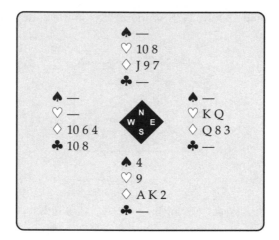

Auken played his last trump and discarded a heart from dummy. If East threw a diamond, declarer would have three diamond tricks. If East let a heart go, declarer would lead a heart to endplay East into leading away from the ◇ Q.

A SIGNAL DEFENCE

It is Teams; dealer South; N/S Vulnerable. You are South, holding this hand:

♠ K 10 8 7 4
♡ A 7 6 5
◇ 5
♣ A 8 3

The bidding starts:

West	North	East	South
			1♠
2♠			

East-West are playing 'Michaels' cue-bids.

What does West's 2♠ show?

Answer: Normally a weakish hand with at least five hearts and an undisclosed five-card, or longer, minor suit. The aim is to locate a useful sacrifice if partner has a good fit for one of the suits.

West	North	East	South
			1♠
2♠	4♡		

North's 4♡ is a splinter. What does it show?

Answer: The splinter bid shows enough high card values for game with at least four trumps and a singleton or void in the suit bid.

West	North	East	South
			1♠
2♠	4♡	5♣	

5♣ is explained as 'pass-or-correct'.

What does that mean?

Answer: West is to pass if the minor suit held is clubs, otherwise remove 5♣ to 5◇.

What action should South take over 5♣?

Answer: As North has a singleton or void in hearts, North figures to hold at least two clubs. You can thus plan an easy defence against 5♣.

What is this defence?

Answer: Lead your singleton diamond, take the first round of trumps, cash the ♡A, give North a heart ruff and receive a diamond ruff. Then take whatever other tricks there are. Therefore you should double 5♣.

West	North	East	South
			1♠
2♠	4♡	5♣	Dbl
5◇	Pass	Pass	?

What has happened now? Are you required to bid on?

Answer: West has diamonds as his minor suit and North's pass indicates no desire to double 5◇ for penalties. East's pass indicates preference for diamonds over hearts. You can thus place East with diamond support (probably at least four cards) and very likely two hearts at most. (With three hearts, East might well have doubled 4♡ rather than choosing the 5♣ bid.)

Now if East has two hearts and North has at most one and you have four, it follows that West will be at least 6-5 in the red suits.

You are required to take some action since North's pass is forcing. The 4♡ splinter showed game values and therefore you cannot let the opponents play in 5◇ undoubled. Either double or bid on.

Which is it?

Answer: You should be able to defeat 5◇ on sheer strength, but it may not be enough to compensate you for the vulnerable game your way. If you were on lead, it would be attractive to double since you know to lead the ♡A and give North a heart ruff. However, North is on lead and may not lead the singleton heart. If North were to lead a spade against 5◇ doubled and West is void in spades (quite possible, given the 6-5 pattern), West might be able to draw North's trumps and there would be no defensive ruff.

You therefore bid on rather than double.

What bid do you choose?

Answer: Another reason to bid on is that the North hand may be quite strong but without first- or second-round control in diamonds. In that case, since you have a singleton diamond, 6♠ might well be possible.

Therefore you should bid 5♡ as a cue-bid, showing the ♡A and suggesting slam possibilities.

West	North	East	South
			1♠
2♠	4♡	5♣	Dbl
5◇	Pass	Pass	5♡
Pass	5♠	Pass	?

What now?

Answer: Partner's 5♠ indicates a minimum splinter hand and your hand is not strong enough to justify pushing on to slam yourself.

The lead is the ♡K and this is what you see:

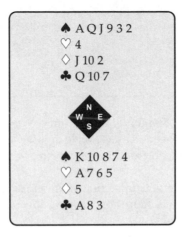

♠ A Q J 9 3 2
♡ 4
♢ J 10 2
♣ Q 10 7

♠ K 10 8 7 4
♡ A 7 6 5
♢ 5
♣ A 8 3

What do you do after taking the ♡A?

Answer: You are bound to lose one diamond and at least one club. Given that West is likely to be 6-5 in the red suits, West figures to have only one or two clubs. That in turn means that East has five or six clubs which are likely to include the king and jack.

In that case, your best chance is to try to endplay East and force a club lead away from his honour holding.

How do you propose to set up an endplay against East?

Answer: You need to eliminate the hearts and the diamonds as well as draw trumps. If East does have K-J-9-x-x in clubs, you can then lead a club to dummy's ten; when East wins, East will have to lead a club back (which you will duck to dummy's ♣Q) or give you a ruff-and-discard.

How can the defence thwart this plan?

Answer: If West gains the lead in diamonds, a club switch will destroy the endplay.

Can you stop West gaining the lead?

Answer: If West has the ◇ A, the ◇ K, or the ◇ Q, you cannot legitimately prevent West gaining the lead, but you can make it tough for the defenders in two ways.

What are they?

Answer: Firstly, lead diamonds from dummy rather than from hand. If East's diamonds are headed by ace-king or just the ace, East might play high on a diamond lead from dummy for fear that you might score a singleton honour.

Secondly, do not draw trumps first. If void in spades, West can signal in diamonds and thus help East to play low on the first round of diamonds from dummy.

At trick two you should ruff a heart in dummy and lead a diamond from table.

This was the full deal which arose in the open semi-finals of the 1996 Olympiad:

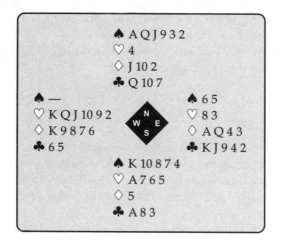

In France *vs* Chinese Taipei, the Chinese South in 5♠ doubled won the heart lead and led a spade to dummy (the ◇ 6 encouraging from West) to play a diamond. Christian Mari, East, played low and West, Marc Bompis, won with the ◇ K and duly switched to a club. Declarer could no longer avoid losing two clubs. One down, -200, and +7 IMPs to France as they were +100 defending against 5♡ doubled at the other table.

In Denmark vs Indonesia, one table bid 1♠ – 4♡ by West – 4♠ – End, and the Indonesian declarer had no problem in making ten tricks for +620.

At the other table, the auction was as given above and the Danish declarer, Lars Blakset, won the heart lead and ruffed a heart in dummy, West playing the two as a count card. He then led the ◊ J from dummy. East rose with the ◊ A and led a trump, but Blakset won this in hand and cross-ruffed two hearts and two diamonds before drawing the last trump. This was the ending:

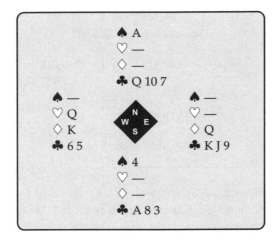

A club to the ♣ 10 and ♣ J endplayed East.

How could the defence have done better?

Answer: West might have played the ♡ Q on the second round of hearts, an unnecessarily high card as a suit-preference signal for the higher suit, diamonds. Now East might have played low on the ◊ J.

VOYAGE OF DISCOVERY

It is Teams; dealer East; Love All. You are South, holding:

```
♠ 8 3
♡ A 6 2
◇ A 9 7 6 5
♣ A 3 2
```

West	North	East	South
		Pass	1NT
Pass	2♡*	Pass	?

*Transfer to spades

What should South bid?

Answer: The transfer shows at least five spades and the 1NT opener has no right to reject the transfer. South must bid 2♠ on these cards. With a maximum opening and spade support, opener would be allowed to do more to show a good fit.

West	North	East	South
		Pass	1NT
Pass	2♡	Pass	2♠
Pass	4◇		

The 4◇ bid is a splinter, showing self-sufficient spades.

What does that mean?

Answer: It means that partner has at least six spades, strong enough that no more than rag-doubleton support is required, and also has a singleton or a void in diamonds. The bid also indicates slam interest, else North would have rebid with a jump to 4♠.

What should South do now?

Answer: It is enough to bid 4♠ here. If all that partner requires to make slam a strong bet are three aces, partner can ask with 4NT. It is true that there are no wasted values in diamonds if the ace is opposite a singleton, but opposite a void, the ◇ A might have very little worth. You and I would still be on happy terms if you did elect to bid 4♡, a cue-bid showing the ♡ A and interest in a spade slam, but that would be more appropriate with three-card spade support and a doubleton in hearts or clubs.

At the table the more aggressive path was chosen and after North checked on aces, the bidding ended in 6♠.

The opening lead is the ♡ 8 and this is what you see:

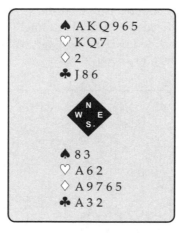

♠ A K Q 9 6 5
♡ K Q 7
◇ 2
♣ J 8 6

♠ 8 3
♡ A 6 2
◇ A 9 7 6 5
♣ A 3 2

This is not a great slam, needing not only spades 3-2 but a lucky position in clubs.

What genuine chances can you see?

Answer: With one more entry to your hand, you could have set up an extra diamond winner in your hand to discard a club from dummy if the diamonds are 4-3. However, with only two entries outside diamonds, you could set up your fifth diamond but you could not return to your hand to cash it.

Assuming the spades are favourable, you can succeed if either opponent has the doubleton ♣K-Q, or East has the ♣K or the ♣Q singleton. If you cash the ♣A and East does play the ♣K or the ♣Q, you will need to know, or guess correctly, whether it is singleton (play the jack on the second round when West plays low) or from K-Q doubleton (duck the second round). A further chance exists if West has both the ♣K and the ♣Q and no more than two diamonds, something like this:

♠ x x x ♡ 9 8 x ◇ x x ♣ K Q x x x

You could win the heart lead in dummy, draw trumps, cash the ◇ A, ruff a diamond and play the hearts, ending in your hand. With West down to clubs only, you lead a low club to endplay West.

Is this a likely layout?

Answer: Not very probable. A 5-2 split in diamonds is against the odds and West having the doubleton reduces those odds by half again. In addition, with clubs headed by K-Q, West might have chosen the club lead instead of a heart. Indeed, the ♣K lead would have made this a respectable slam instead of an awful one.

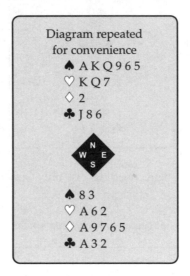

Diagram repeated
for convenience
♠ A K Q 9 6 5
♡ K Q 7
◇ 2
♣ J 8 6

♠ 8 3
♡ A 6 2
◇ A 9 7 6 5
♣ A 3 2

How do you start the play?

Answer: Win the lead in dummy and start on trumps. All follow to two rounds (phew!) and on the third spade, West discards a club.

How does that affect your thinking?

Answer: With West short in spades, it is now less likely that West is also short in diamonds.

What next?

Answer: It costs you nothing to play diamonds and see what happens. All follow low on your diamond to the ace and when you continue with the ◇ 5, West plays the ◇ 8 and East the ◇ 10. The time has now come to commit yourself to one line of play or the other.

Which do you choose?

Answer: West's choice of the ♡ 8 opening lead, which looks as though it is from a short suit, doubleton or tripleton probably, plus the fact that West has the shorter holding in spades and West's failure to lead the ♣ K if that suit were headed by K-Q, all combine to make an endplay on West a very unlikely hope. Your better chance is to find East with either ♣ K-Q doubleton, or the ♣ K or the ♣ Q singleton.

Why will West not hold ♣ K-Q doubleton?

Answer: Since West has discarded a club, you can forget about West being down to K-Q bare.

How do you continue?

Answer: Before you start on the clubs, you may as well find out as much as you can about the lie of the red suits. Even if luck is with you, it will still be essential to know whether East started with a singleton club or ♣ K-Q doubleton.

You cash ♡ K; West discards another club.

What do you know now?

Answer: This is only the second round of hearts and so West began with a singleton heart and East with six hearts.

What do you know so far about East?

Answer: We have just discovered that East started with six hearts and we noted earlier that East held three spades originally. As East has followed to two diamonds, we now know eleven of East's cards.

What next?

Answer: You continue your voyage of discovery with a heart to the ace and ruff a third round of diamonds. East follows to the third diamond.

What does this tell you?

Answer: Having an initial holding of three spades, six hearts and three diamonds, East will either be singleton or void in clubs. You will have to pray it is a singleton top honour.

When you lead a club, East plays the ♣Q. Oh, joy, oh, rapture. You win with the ♣A and lead a club back, rising with the jack when West plays low.

The deal comes from the 1998 world championships. In the semi-finals of the Rosenblum (open teams), all four North-South pairs stopped in game. So did one table in the final of the McConnell Cup (women's teams). At the other table, 6♠ was reached and the full deal looked like this:

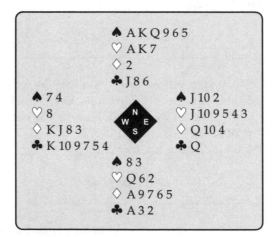

In practice, South opened a mini-1NT, showing 10-12 points, but in order to discuss the bidding sensibly for standard Acol bidders, I interchanged the ♡ A and the ♡ Q. This had no effect on the play of the hand.

The declarer was Daniela von Arnim who produced the winning line as described, and landed the slam to pick up 11 lucky IMPs for her team.

It is true that on the actual cards, the slam is a poor bet but there are many South hands in the 10-12 point range that would make 6♠ virtually a lay-down. Any of these South hands produce excellent chances for twelve tricks:

Hand A	*Hand B*	*Hand C*	*Hand D*
♠ 8 3 2	♠ J 3 2	♠ J 3 2	♠ 8 3 2
♡ Q J 6 2	♡ Q 6 5	♡ 6 5 2	♡ Q 6
◇ A 9 7	◇ 9 7 6 5 3	◇ A 7 6	◇ A 7 6 5 3
♣ A 3 2	♣ A K	♣ K Q 10 4	♣ A 3 2

WELL HANDLED BY HANLON

It is Teams; dealer South; E/W Vulnerable. You are South, holding:

♠ Q J 4 2
♡ K Q 7 2
◇ A J 10
♣ 7 5

Playing Acol, what is your opening bid?

Answer: Despite the weakness in clubs, it is imperative to open 1NT, 12-14 balanced. If you are too frightened to do this, adopt some other system.

A worthless doubleton is no bar to a 1NT opening. If you fail to open 1NT with such hands you will seriously mislead partner with whatever other sequence you adopt.

The bidding continues:

West	North	East	South
			1NT
Pass	2♣	Pass	?

What now?

Answer: When holding both majors, it is standard to show the hearts first in reply to 2♣ Stayman.

The bidding concludes:

West	North	East	South
			1NT
Pass	2♣	Pass	2♡
Pass	4♡	All Pass	

The lead is the ♠ A and when dummy appears, this is what you see:

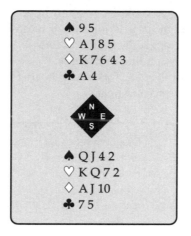

On the ♠ A, East plays the ♠ 3, and at trick two West switches to the ♣ 6.

Your move?

Answer: There is no benefit in ducking. If hearts behave and you can pick up the diamond suit, you might avoid losing a club trick altogether.

You rise with the ♣ A and East plays the ♣ 10, encouraging.

What now?

Answer: There is no reason to delay the trump suit.

How do you plan to play the trump suit?
Is there any reason to choose a particular order in which to draw trumps?

Answer: The play in the trump suit is related to the suit you intend to play next, diamonds.

What is the best technical play in the diamond suit?

Answer: Missing the queen it is normal to finesse on the second round (cash one top honour first in case the queen is singleton). However,

---

with K-J-10 opposite A-x-x-x-x or A-J-10 opposite K-x-x-x-x, a first-round finesse, low to the jack, is superior as it caters for Q-x-x-x onside. As you may need to repeat the diamond finesse, you should start with two rounds of trumps, ending in dummy.

You therefore cash the ♡K and lead a heart to dummy's ace. West discards a club on the second heart.

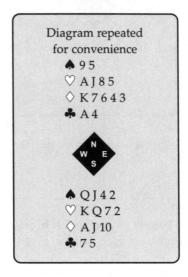

Diagram repeated
for convenience
♠ 9 5
♡ A J 8 5
◇ K 7 6 4 3
♣ A 4

♠ Q J 4 2
♡ K Q 7 2
◇ A J 10
♣ 7 5

How does the 4-1 break affect your plan?

Answer: Holding a singleton heart, West is likely to have length in diamonds and therefore the ◇ Q. You cannot afford to draw all of East's trumps, since a misguess in diamonds will see the opponents cashing a lot of clubs and a spade trick.

What about tackling the diamonds next?

Answer: This is also very risky. If you play a diamond to the ace and then run the ◇ J, two bad things might happen. If West began with four diamonds, East will ruff the second round, put West in with a spade, and score a second diamond ruff. If East began with Q-x in diamonds, the diamond finesse loses, East puts West in with a spade and receives a diamond ruff. Either of these possibilities leaves you two down.

What should you do then?

Answer: You may as well set up a spade trick. Perhaps they will open up the diamonds for you.

You lead the ♠9 to your queen. West takes the ♠K and leads the ♣9 to East's ♣Q. You have lost three tricks. East returns the ♡10.

Where do you win this?

Answer: Your remaining trumps are J-8 opposite Q-7 and East will have the ♡9 left after this trick. You cannot afford to win in hand and ruff a spade: that gives East a trump trick. You cannot afford to win in dummy, come to hand with a diamond to the ace and ruff a spade: that strands you in dummy with an almost certain loser in diamonds.

You win the heart in hand and turn your attention to diamonds. You intend to finesse against West for the ◊Q.

How do you plan to do that?

Answer: You need to sneak a diamond past West if he has three or four diamonds. If you play the ◊J and West covers, there is no way back to dummy's diamonds unless East started with three diamonds. You therefore lead the ◊10. West plays low.

Do you continue with your plan and run the ◊10,
or do you change your mind and play East for ◊Q?

Answer: It is true that West has erred by not covering the ◊10 but for all West knows, East has the ◊J and to cover could be a serious blunder. Since you are playing West for diamond length, you should stick by your original plan and run the ◊10.

It wins the trick.

What now?

Answer: You must not play a second round of diamonds. If they are 4-1, all your good work so far is undone. East will ruff and you are one down. If the diamonds are 3-2, you are home by drawing the last trump.

You play a heart to the jack and make the hand, even though the diamonds were 4-1 all along. This was the complete deal from the 1996 World Open Teams Olympiad (diagram overleaf):

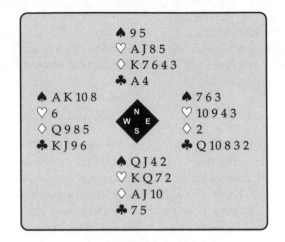

In New Zealand *vs* Indonesia, both Souths were in 4♡. Ken Yule (New Zealand) made it after a spade lead, but no club switch at trick two. Lasut (Indonesia) went one down after a top spade lead (discouraged) and a club switch when he tested trumps and then played a diamond to the ◊ J and the ◊ Q. Tom Hanlon for Ireland *vs* Croatia made it on the line described so far.

After the ♠ A, low club switch won by the ace, the ♡ K, the ♡ A, spade to queen and king, club to the queen, heart exit won by the queen, the ◊ 10 run successfully, the end-position was:

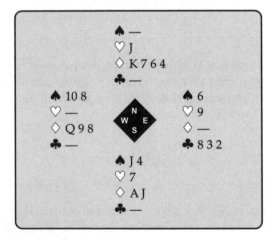

When Hanlon led a trump to dummy's jack, West was squeezed in spades and diamonds. Had West covered the ◊ 10 with the queen, the squeeze would have failed as dummy would be out of entries.

A FISTFUL OF DIAMONDS

It is Teams; dealer East; Love All. You are South, holding:

♠ J 9 6 3
♡ Q 7 4
♢ 9 6
♣ J 10 4 3

The bidding starts:

West	North	East	South
		1♠	Pass
Pass	Dbl	Pass	?

What should South do?

Answer: The choices are 2♣ or 1NT. A reply of 1NT to a take-out double is commonly played as 6-9 points. You might fudge to 5 points but a mere 4 count is quite some fudge. The danger in bidding 1NT is that partner becomes excited with no-trumps and, placing you with at least 6 points, raises to 2NT or 3NT.

It is far better to bid 2♣, which does not promises any points at all. In the words from Porgy & Bess, you got plenty o' nothin'.

West	North	East	South
		1♠	Pass
Pass	Dbl	Pass	2♣
Pass	3♣	Pass	?

What now?

Answer: The raise to 3♣ is strong and invites game, but your hand is still not strong enough to justify further action. Pass.

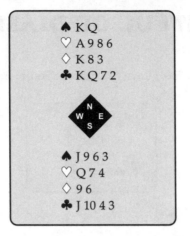

♠ K Q
♡ A 9 8 6
◇ K 8 3
♣ K Q 7 2

♠ J 9 6 3
♡ Q 7 4
◇ 9 6
♣ J 10 4 3

Against 3♣ West leads the ♠7 and East wins with the ace. The ♠4 is returned, West following with the ♠2 and dummy wins.

What is the spade position?

_____

Answer: West has played the ♠7, then the ♠2, showing a doubleton and so East began with ♠ A-10-8-5-4.

Has anything else struck you about the play so far?

_____

Answer: At trick two, East returned the lowest spade, the ♠4. As East could afford the ♠8 or the ♠5, the lowest spade should be a suit-preference signal for the lowest suit, excluding trumps. This means that East is strong in diamonds. You can expect East's diamonds to be headed by A-Q. With a desire for hearts, East would have returned the ♠8.

What do you play now?

_____

Answer: There is no reason to delay trumps and so you play the ♣K next. East wins with the ace and plays a third spade. You play ♠9 and West ruffs with ♣9. You overruff in dummy.

What now?

Answer: Draw the missing trumps. A low club to the jack does that. You cash the ♠ J, on which West discards a diamond, and you pitch a diamond from dummy, leaving:

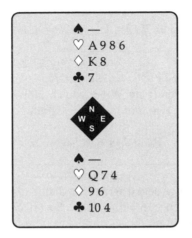

What do you know about the East hand?

Answer: East began with five spades and two clubs. That leaves six red cards. East has turned up with two black aces, and has suggested strength in diamonds.

You have lost two tricks so far and are sure to lose at least one heart. If East has the ♡ K and West the ◇ A, you will lose only two more tricks but the ◇ A is almost certainly with East. If West has the ♡ K, there is no hope.

Can you see any chance if East has the ♡K as well as the ◇A?

Answer: Continue with the ♡ A and a second heart. If East has ♡ K-x-x, you can score an extra heart trick to discard a diamond from hand Even if East began with the ♡ K doubleton (a 5-2-4-2 pattern), East will have to play diamonds for you, or give you a ruff-and-discard after winning the second heart. In either case, one diamond loser disappears.

You cash the ♡ A and East plays the ♡ K.

What do you make of that?

Answer: Perhaps East began with the ♡K singleton? That's unlikely. That would give East a 5-1-5-2 pattern and with good diamonds as well as the two black aces, East would almost certainly have bid 2♢ over North's double.

> *What is going on if East does not have a singleton heart?*

Answer: East may well have worked out your plan and has unblocked the ♡K to escape the endplay. When you continue with a second heart, East follows with the two and you win with the queen.

> *What does East have left?*

Answer: East probably began with four diamonds and in addition has one spade left. If East began with ♡K-J-2, East may well have continued to unblock with the ♡J on the second heart (you would have let the ♡J hold). You cannot entirely dismiss the chance that East made a bluff unblock from ♡K-x-x but if so you had no winning move after East unblocked the ♡K.

> *Assuming East did begin with ♡K-2 doubleton, how do you proceed?*

Answer: You cannot afford to play a third heart. West will win and lead a diamond and you will be one down. You have to try to endplay East in diamonds. Small to the king will work if East started with ♢A-Q-J-10 but not if East has any lesser holding. If you play a diamond to the king and East has ♢A-Q-J-x, ♢A-Q-10-x, or ♢A-J-10-x, East can win and play a low diamond next to West, who will cash a heart for one down.

You can succeed as long as West has only one honour out of the ♢Q, ♢J or ♢10. Lead the ♢6 and if West follows low, insert dummy's eight; the ♢6 is better than the ♢9, just in case West has ♢J-10-x-x and carelessly plays low on the ♢6 (whereas West is more likely to cover the ♢9).

This plan succeeds. East captures the ♢8, cashes the ♢A but then has to give you a ruff-and-discard, and away goes your loser in hearts.

The full deal, which arose in Round 7 of the 2000 Orbis Venice Cup match between Denmark and France, was:

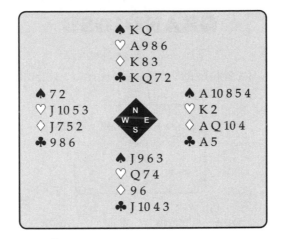

The bidding and play went exactly as described with declarer Kirsten Steen-Møller making nine tricks in clubs for +110 via the neat endplay in diamonds, despite the fine unblocking move in hearts by Veronique Bessis of France. The seven-card ending was:

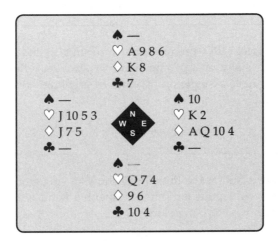

An important principle applies to the bidding and opening lead. Had East bid 2◊ over North's double, West should lead a diamond rather than a spade and that will defeat 3♣. When partner passes your opening bid, do not bid a second suit if you would prefer partner to lead your first suit. If a spade lead is wanted, East should pass over the double. As the diamonds are much stronger than the spades, the 2◊ bid is worth the risk.

GRANDIOSE

It is Teams; dealer South; E/W Vulnerable. You are South, holding:

♠ K Q J 10 4 2
♡ A J 10
♦ K 9
♣ Q 5

West	North	East	South
			1♠
Pass	2NT		

You are playing the Jacoby 2NT convention.

What does North's response mean?

Answer: The Jacoby 2NT promises four-card support and enough points for game (normally an opening hand or stronger). Responder will almost never have a singleton or void, as a splinter response would then be used.

How is opener expected to rebid?

Answer: A new suit at the three level shows a singleton or void, and bidding 4♠ would show a minimum opening hand with at least five spades and no void, no singleton.

What do you bid?

Answer: 3NT would show extra values in a balanced hand with four spades, and so you should bid 3♠. This shows extra length in spades, more than a minimum opening and no singleton or void.

West	North	East	South
			1♠
Pass	2NT	Pass	3♠
Pass	4♣	Pass	4♡
Pass	4NT	Pass	?

4♣ and 4♡ are cue-bids showing the ace in the suit bid. 4NT is Roman Key-Card Blackwood.

What is your reply?

Answer: In Roman Key-Card Blackwood, you show not only aces but also the king and queen of trumps.

You bid 5♠ to show two key cards (the ♡ A and the ♠ K) plus the ♠ Q as well.

West	North	East	South
			1♠
Pass	2NT	Pass	3♠
Pass	4♣	Pass	4♡
Pass	4NT	Pass	5♠
No	5NT	No	6♢
No	6♡	No	?

5NT promised that all key cards are held and asked for specific kings (by partnership agreement) and 6♢ showed the ♢ K.

Partner's 6♡ now asks you to bid the grand slam if you hold the ♡ K.

What do you bid?

Answer: Since you do not hold ♡ K, the simple answer is that you should sign off in 6♠. On the other hand, North could easily hold ♣ A-K-x and ♢ A-Q-x, which would allow you to discard your heart losers. Likewise, if North has ♣ A-K-J-x, your heart losers vanish. As North cannot know about your ♣ Q, perhaps that is just as good as the ♡ K.

At the table, judging that the grand slam should not be any worse than a finesse and could be lay-down, declarer elected to bid 7♠ despite the absence of the ♡ K.

Against 7♠, West leads the ♢ 4 and you see (diagram overleaf):

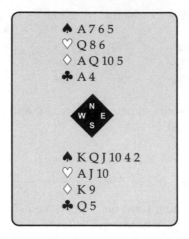

♠ A 7 6 5
♡ Q 8 6
♢ A Q 10 5
♣ A 4

♠ K Q J 10 4 2
♡ A J 10
♢ K 9
♣ Q 5

You play low from dummy, East contributes the ♢ 7 and you win with your ♢ 9. You draw trumps in three rounds, West discarding three clubs.

What is your plan from here?

Answer: The best chance is to cash the ♢ K, cross to dummy with a trump, discard a heart and a club on dummy's diamond winners and then take the heart finesse.

All follow to the ♢ K. When you lead a spade to dummy, West discards another club and East throws a low heart. On the ♢ A, you throw the ♡ 10, East follows low, and West plays the ♢ J.

Has anything happened to affect your play?

Answer: It appears that West's opening lead was from ♢ J-x-x. Whether it was from J-x-x or from J-x-x-x, this is a very risky lead. It could easily cost the crucial trick if partner has Q-x-x or similar.

Against a grand slam, one leads as safely as possible. If you were West and held ♡ x-x-x and ♢ J-x-x, which suit would you lead? Of course, a heart. Since West has chosen the risky diamond lead, it is a reasonable inference that West does not have a worthless holding in hearts. As you hold all the other honours in hearts, it follows that West has the ♡ K and that the heart finesse will fail.

Similar logic suggests that West does not have a safe club lead either.

If the heart finesse will fail, what other hope is there?

Answer: If West began with the ♣K as well as the ♡K, you will be able to squeeze West in those suits by means of a Vienna Coup.

How does a Vienna Coup operate?

Answer: Declarer cashes a winner to establish a winner for an opponent and then proceeds to squeeze the opponent out of that trick.

In this case, you play dummy's ◊Q and discard the ♡J. You then cross to your ♡A, setting up the king for West, and then play off the rest of your trumps.

The successful declarer was Seamus Browne who won the Brilliancy Prize (shared) for his play on this deal from the 1999 Australian National Open Teams Championship:

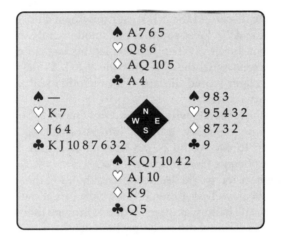

Browne reached this ending (diagram overleaf):

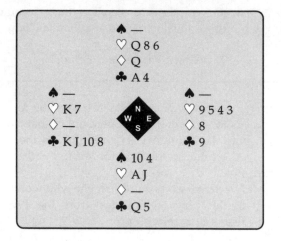

On the ◇ Q, he discarded the ♡ J, West throwing a club, and crossed to the ♡ A. On the ♠ 10, West could afford another club and the ♡ 8 was discarded from dummy. When Browne led his last trump, West had a choice of poisons with the ♡ K and the ♣ K-J. Whichever suit was discarded, declarer would discard from the other suit in dummy and score the last two tricks.

One can only speculate why West did not enter the bidding. Despite unfavourable vulnerabilty, a weak jump-overcall of 3♣ or a pre-emptive jump to 4♣ would be an acceptable action. Even 2♣ may inhibit the opponents from bidding to 7♠.

As for the decision to bid 7♠ despite not holding the ♡ K, if you can play the cards as well as Browne does, you can allow yourself such liberties. After the hand was over, no doubt Browne thought to himself, 'I felt the grand slam would be better than just a finesse.'

INCURABLE OPTIMISM
REWARDED

It is Teams; dealer South; Game All. As South, you hold:

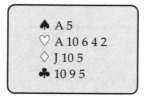

West	North	East	South
			Pass
Pass	1◇	2♠ *	?

*Weak jump overcall, 6+ suit, 6-10 HCP

What should you bid now?

Answer: The values are skimpy for a 3♡ reply in normal circumstances and partner is a third-hand opener. Still, you are entitled to bid 3♡ here for two reasons.

What are they?

Answer: First, you are a passed hand and so your 3♡ bid is not forcing. Second, the bidding indicates that partner probably has a strong hand and is not a light third-seat opener. West could not open and East has made a weak, pre-emptive bid. Therefore, partner is likely to be strong.
The bidding continues:

West	North	East	South
			Pass
Pass	1◇	2♠	3♡
Pass	5♡	Pass	?

What does partner's 5♡ bid mean? What action do you take now?

Answer: A jump-raise to five-of-a-major usually asks you to bid six if your trumps are strong. If that were the meaning here, you would pass 5♡. However, when there has been an opposition bid, the jump-raise to five-of-a-major is used to ask for control of the opponents' suit. The 5♡ bid here says, 'If you can control the spades, bid six; if not, please pass.'

Since you have the ♠A, you bid 6♡.

The lead is the ♠7, and dummy reveals that partner is either an incurable optimist, or has incredible faith in your declarer technique:

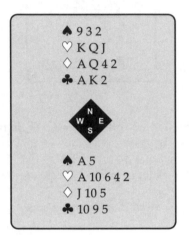

```
        ♠ 9 3 2
        ♡ K Q J
        ◇ A Q 4 2
        ♣ A K 2

              N
           W     E
              S

        ♠ A 5
        ♡ A 10 6 4 2
        ◇ J 10 5
        ♣ 10 9 5
```

East plays ♠10.

Your move?

Answer: Do not even consider ducking this. It is possible (but unlikely) that East has seven spades and if so, your ♠A would be ruffed on the next round.

There is no reason to delay drawing trumps and so you continue with a low heart to the king, and the ♡Q next, all following. When you play the ♡J, East contributes the last outstanding trump.

What do you do now?

Answer: There is no escaping the diamond finesse and so you should overtake the ♡J with the ace. West discards a diamond on this. When you play the ◇10, West plays the ◇7, you close your eyes, say a little prayer and play low from dummy.

When you open your eyes, the ◇ 10 has won the trick, East playing the ◇ 8. You continue with the ◇ J, West covers with the ◇ K. Dummy's ace wins and East discards a spade.

Pity about that. Had the diamonds been 3-3, you would have been all right.

What do know so far about East's shape?

Answer: East began with three hearts and one diamond (proven) and probably six or seven spades. (A weak jump-overcall with a strong five-card suit opposite a passed hand is not unheard of, but it holds less appeal when one is vulnerable.)

You have eleven tricks via five hearts, one spade, three diamonds and two clubs, but it seems as though you have an unavoidable spade loser and a club loser.

Can you see any prospect at all for producing a twelfth trick?

Answer: The only chance is a squeeze against West. There are two possibilities. If East began with seven spades and so has a 7-3-1-2 pattern, then West has to guard both the diamonds and the clubs, and your plan is to squeeze West. If East's pattern is 6-3-1-3, you can still squeeze West in the minors if West has both the ♣ Q and the ♣ J. That is not a great chance but it is the only one you have.

You are in dummy.

What do you play at trick seven?

Answer: Since you need to return to your hand to play off your trumps and you also need to concede a trick to the opposition (to 'rectify the count' for the squeeze), you must now play a spade from dummy.

The complete deal looks like this (diagram overleaf):

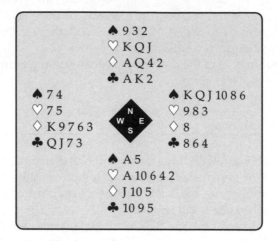

After you play a spade from dummy, East wins and the position now is:

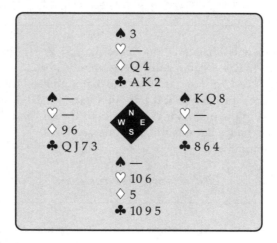

The deal arose in the 1997 Venice Cup (the women's world teams championship). At this point East exited with a club to the ten, jack and ace. Declarer then ruffed the spade to hand and West discarded a club.

This was the position with four cards to go:

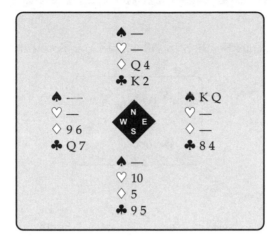

When declarer led the ♡10, West had to concede. Whichever minor West discards, declarer discards low from the other minor in dummy and makes the last three tricks. The successful declarer was Tobi Sokolow of USA 1, gaining 13 IMPs as the other table stopped in 4♡, making five.

USA1 went on to take the title by beating China in the final by 249-184 IMPs.

A GOOD IMPRESSION

It is Teams; dealer South; N/S Vulnerable. You, South, hold:

♠ A Q 3
♡ A K 8 5 2
◇ A 10 5
♣ 10 3

The bidding starts:

West	North	East	South
			1♣ [1]
3◇ [2]	Pass	Pass	?

[1] Strong Club system
[2] Pre-emptive

What action should you take now?

Answer: When you play a strong club system, you are likely to encounter plenty of pre-empts.

You treat the auction as though the pre-empt were the opening bid and act accordingly. Had it gone (3◇) – Pass – (Pass), you would choose between 3♡ and 3NT, with most players preferring 3♡ (as it allows a raise, or a 3♠ bid, from partner). Double is not attractive because you have length in diamonds, and if partner bids 3♠ or 4♠ you could easily have a 5-3 fit in hearts, but only a 4-3 fit in spades.

With 5-3 in the majors, you will usually do better by bidding a good five-card suit.

The auction proceeds:

West	North	East	South
			1♣
3◇	Pass	Pass	3♡
Pass	4♡	All Pass	

The lead is the ◇ 2 and this is what you see:

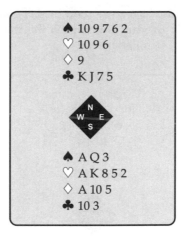

♠ 10 9 7 6 2
♡ 10 9 6
♢ 9
♣ K J 7 5

N
W E
S

♠ A Q 3
♡ A K 8 5 2
♢ A 10 5
♣ 10 3

Clearly you must have impressed partner with your declarer prowess recently. If you make this contract, you will impress not only partner and the opponents but yourself, too.

What can you deduce from the ♢ 2 lead?

Answer: The ♢ 2 is an abnormal lead, obviously not fourth highest. Preempters choose such leads to carry a suit-preference message. Here the ♢ 2, the lowest card, asks for the lowest suit, clubs.

Why would that be?

Answer: West is hoping that East might win the lead and return a club. The reason is that West is void in clubs.

What can you deduce about the hand patterns so far?

Answer: West should have seven diamonds and, if your assumption about the club void is correct, West figures to hold a 3-3-7-0 pattern. No one will underwrite that holding, but it is a sound policy not to pre-empt with a four-card major. If West has adhered to that advice and does not have a four-card major, then a 3-3-7-0 distribution is very likely.

East can be placed with two diamonds and seven clubs headed by the ace and queen. If West began with a 3-3-7-0, then East is 2-2-2-7. You are staring at a probable spade loser, a probable heart loser, two club losers, and you also have to be concerned about your last diamond, as East can probably overruff dummy on the third round. Clearly a prayer or two will not go amiss here.

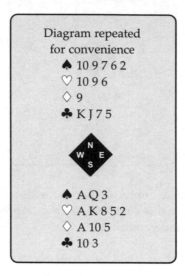

Diagram repeated
for convenience
♠ 10 9 7 6 2
♡ 10 9 6
◇ 9
♣ K J 7 5

♠ A Q 3
♡ A K 8 5 2
◇ A 10 5
♣ 10 3

East plays the ◇ Q on the opening lead and you take it with the ace. You cash the ♡ A and East drops ♡ J.

What do you make of that?

Answer: If East began with Q-J doubleton in hearts, your first miracle has arrived. You continue with the ♡ K – and sure enough, Lady Luck is with you, East plays the ♡ Q.

How do you continue?

Answer: It is time to take a diamond ruff in dummy, followed by a spade finesse. If East also began with K-J doubleton in spades, you are going to make twelve tricks and can ask why partner did not bid more.

The diamond ruff fetches the ◇ 4 from East and when you play a spade, East plays the ♠8. Your ♠Q wins, and West plays the ♠ 4.

What next?

Answer: You should draw the last trump with your ♡ 8, and cash the ♠ A, on which East plays the ♠ K.

You have five heart tricks, two spades, the ◊ A and a diamond ruff for nine tricks, but you still have a spade loser, a diamond loser and two club losers.

How do you propose to deal with that?

Answer: Given your assumption about West's void in clubs, East will have only clubs left.

This was the case on the actual deal from the semi-finals of the 1998 Australian National Open Teams Championship:

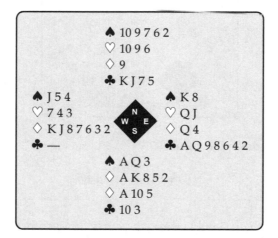

```
                ♠ 10 9 7 6 2
                ♡ 10 9 6
                ◊ 9
                ♣ K J 7 5
  ♠ J 5 4                      ♠ K 8
  ♡ 7 4 3          N           ♡ Q J
  ◊ K J 8 7 6 3 2  W   E       ◊ Q 4
  ♣ —                S         ♣ A Q 9 8 6 4 2
                ♠ A Q 3
                ◊ A K 8 5 2
                ◊ A 10 5
                ♣ 10 3
```

You lead the ♣ 10. East can take two club tricks, but must give you at least one club for your tenth trick.

Everyone stands and applauds.

UNION JACK

It is Teams; dealer West; N/S Vulnerable. The bidding goes:

West	North	East	South
Pass	1◇ *	Pass	1♡
Pass	1♠	Pass	2NT
All Pass			

*Precision, need not have diamonds

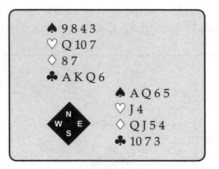

```
          ♠ 9 8 4 3
          ♡ Q 10 7
          ◇ 8 7
          ♣ A K Q 6
                        ♠ A Q 6 5
                        ♡ J 4
               N        ◇ Q J 5 4
            W     E      ♣ 10 7 3
               S
```

You are East, defending against 2NT. West leads the ♠J.

Which card do you play?

_____

Answer: First, you should be asking yourself a few other questions.

How many points is South likely to have?

_____

Answer: As 1◇ is 11-15 and 2NT invites game, South figures to have 11-12 points.

What does that leave for West?

_____

Answer: Dummy has 11, you have 10 and South 11-12. That is 32-33, leaving partner with 7-8 points.

What is South's club holding?

Answer: South should have a club stopper for the jump to 2NT. As dummy has A-K-Q-6 in clubs, South's stopper should be J-x-x-x or longer, and as South bid 1♡ initially, we can place South with at least 4-4 in hearts and clubs.

Partner has led the ♠J, an unusual choice in that it is dummy's bid suit.

Which holdings are consistent with the ♠J lead?

Answer: Partner's ♠J could be:

(a) a singleton
(b) top of a doubleton
(c) top from J-10-x
(d) top of an interior sequence, K-J-10-x
(e) top from J-10-7-2

Which of these can you eliminate?

Answer: It cannot be a singleton lead. That would give South four spades and South would have chosen a spade raise, not 2NT.

Top from J-10-7-2 is unlikely. That is not an attractive holding to lead in a suit bid by dummy and if one were to lead it, it would be preferable to lead fourth-highest, not the jack. When leading through dummy's suit, a short suit lead is preferable to a lead from length.

When will it gain to play the ace?

Answer: The ace gains in only one case, when West has led from J-10-7-2, which is unlikely. If partner has led from J-x or J-10-x, South will make the king whether you play the ace or play low. Playing the ace may block the suit if partner has led from J-10-x and therefore you ought to play low.

Unless partner started with A-x-x-x-x in diamonds, you will be unable to defeat 2NT by winning with your ♠A and switching to diamonds now. Given the nebulous nature of the 1◇ opening, partner might well have led a diamond from a five-card holding. If declarer takes the ♠K, you need to hope that partner gains the lead in hearts, continues the spades and then you can switch to diamonds.

You do play low on the ♠J, which wins the trick. Partner continues with the ♠K.

Answer: It appears that partner started with an interior sequence in spades, perhaps ♠ K-J-10. Partner will not hold the ♠ K-J doubleton for, if he had chosen that lead, he would have started with the king. Accordingly, you play low on the next spade as well. To your surprise, declarer follows with the ♠ 10 but all is well as partner continues with the ♠ 2.

You can now place declarer with a probable pattern of 2-4-3-4. You win with the ♠ Q and cash the ♠ A. Declarer has discarded two clubs, while partner discards the ♡ 2, a discouraging signal, on the fourth spade. You did not really need that signal, since it was clear that a heart switch cannot be useful. You are about to shift to diamonds.

Which diamond?

Answer: If partner has a top heart and the ◇ K it will not matter which diamond you choose but if partner has the ◇ A, it can be better to switch to the ◇ Q.

This works out extremely well as you collect four diamond tricks and take the contract three down for +300. The complete deal looked like this:

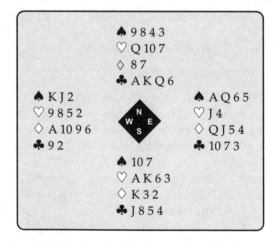

♠ 9 8 4 3
♡ Q 10 7
◇ 8 7
♣ A K Q 6

♠ K J 2
♡ 9 8 5 2
◇ A 10 9 6
♣ 9 2

♠ A Q 6 5
♡ J 4
◇ Q J 5 4
♣ 10 7 3

♠ 10 7
♡ A K 6 3
◇ K 3 2
♣ J 8 5 4

It takes a spade lead to beat 2NT and West did well to start unblocking with the ♠ J. The ♠ K lead can also work but when the ♠ J is continued,

East might well overtake in order to switch to diamonds and that would cost a trick.

In a qualifying-round match between Great Britain and USA 1 in the 1991 Bermuda Bowl, the British West led the ♠J but East won with the ♠A and returned a low spade to the king. Reluctant to set up dummy's ♠9 with a spade continuation, West switched to a low diamond and the USA scored a lucky +150 instead of going down for -300.

Great Britain went on to win the match by 58-31 IMPs, 19-11 in VPs.

A TENTH IS ENOUGH

It is Teams; dealer South; N/S Vulnerable. You, South, hold:

> ♠ A K 10
> ♡ K J 5
> ◇ 10 5
> ♣ K Q J 5 2

The bidding starts:

West	North	East	South
			1NT[1]
2♡[2]	2NT	Pass	?

[1] 15-18
[2] Natural

2NT is the Lebensohl Convention.

What should South do?

Answer: After second player bids a suit over 1NT, the Lebensohl 2NT response requires opener to bid 3♣. Responder intends to make a purely competitive bid in a new suit lower-ranking than the overcalled suit, or intends to make a strong bid by continuing with 3NT or by bidding the enemy suit next.

The sequence of 2NT followed by a strong bid is used by many pairs to confirm a stopper in the enemy suit, while the same actions without going through 2NT deny a stopper in the enemy suit. However, in this partnership 2NT followed a strong action is used to deny a stopper in their suit. It matters little which approach you adopt as long as you and partner are on the same wavelength.

Bid 3♣, the rebid forced by 2NT.

The auction continues:

West	North	East	South
			1NT
2♡	2NT	Pass	3♣
3♠ *	3NT	4♡	?
* Natural			

What do you make of the 4♡ bid?

Answer: As your side is vulnerable and they are not, East is taking a sacrifice with a fit for hearts and based on the distributional hand shown by West.

What action do you take over 4♡?

Answer: Partner's 3NT over 3♠ indicates the values for game. You have four possible courses of action: Pass, Double, 5♣ or 4NT.

Pass is reasonable since it is forcing and leaves the decision to partner. Double is because so much of your strength is in the suits bid by the opponents. As partner is very likely to be short in hearts, there is a very strong chance that partner has three or four clubs, and so 5♣ is also reasonable. 4NT has some risk attached; double or 5♣ is safer.

Suppose the complete auction was:

West	North	East	South
			1NT
2♡	2NT	Pass	3♣
3♠	3NT	4♡	4NT
All Pass			

West leads the ♡10 to East's ♡Q, and this is what you see (diagram on next page):

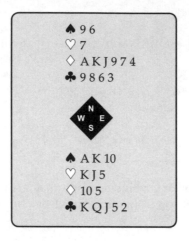

```
        ♠ 9 6
        ♡ 7
        ◇ A K J 9 7 4
        ♣ 9 8 6 3

              N
           W     E
              S

        ♠ A K 10
        ♡ K J 5
        ◇ 10 5
        ♣ K Q J 5 2
```

What action do you take?

Answer: In 3NT there would be a case for ducking to try to sever communications but it is better here to capture the queen. East is likely to hold at least three hearts, and if you duck West can simply duck the heart return to retain communication. It is likely that West's ten lead is from A-10-9, but it is possible that East has A-Q-x and has played the queen to ferret out the king.

If this is the case and you duck, you have turned two tricks into one. You take the ♡ Q with your king.

What do you play next?

Answer: The diamonds might do for nine tricks. Knocking out the ♣ A also leads to nine tricks.

Which minor should you try?

Answer: If you try the clubs and East has the ace, a heart return will finish you at once if West began with A-10-9-x-x or longer. If you try the diamonds and they do not behave, you can revert to clubs later.

OK, so try the diamonds first.

What is the normal play with this combination?

Answer: To finesse against West for the queen without cashing the ace first. If the diamonds were five opposite three, or four-four, cashing the ace first would be right. When the suit is 6-2, finessing on the first round will not cost if the suit breaks 3-2, but if the suit splits 4-1, cashing the ace gains against a singleton queen with East (one time in five) and loses against any other singleton with East (four times out of five). Running the ten on the first round gains in 80% of the 4-1 breaks when East has the singleton.

Is that what you intend to do here?

Answer: Hardly. East cannot have a singleton diamond as West will not hold four diamonds.

Why not?

Answer: Because West has so many cards in the majors.

How many hearts for the 2♡ bid?

Answer: At least five. Then West bid 3♠ over 3♣.

How many spades?

Answer: At least five and therefore six hearts for the previous heart bid. With a 5-4 or 5-5 pattern in the majors, West would have chosen a major-suit take-out over 1NT.

What pattern will West therefore have?

Answer: 5-6-1-1, 5-6-2-0, or 5-6-0-2. That is why there is no point in taking a finesse in diamonds. The diamonds will run only if West began with ♢ Q-x.

You cash ♢ A-K and West very decently obliges by playing the queen on the second round. You therefore place West with a 5-6-2-0 pattern. You can run the rest of the diamonds and your tally, counting the ♡ K at trick one and two spade winners, is now up to nine tricks.

Where will you find the tenth trick?

Answer: If West did start with hearts headed by the ace and spades headed by queen-jack, you can endplay West. This would have worked on the actual deal from the final of the 1978 Venice Cup:

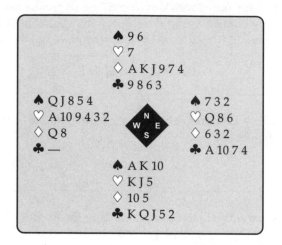

```
                    ♠ 9 6
                    ♡ 7
                    ◇ A K J 9 7 4
                    ♣ 9 8 6 3
    ♠ Q J 8 5 4                      ♠ 7 3 2
    ♡ A 10 9 4 3 2       N           ♡ Q 8 6
    ◇ Q 8            W       E       ◇ 6 3 2
    ♣ —                 S           ♣ A 10 7 4
                    ♠ A K 10
                    ♡ K J 5
                    ◇ 10 5
                    ♣ K Q J 5 2
```

You need to watch West's discards. After running the diamonds, discarding clubs from hand, if West has discarded four hearts, you play West to have come down to the ♡ A bare. Cross to hand with a spade and play a low heart, felling the ace and setting up the ♡ J.

If West discards three hearts only and one spade, coming down to ♠ Q-J-x-x and ♡ A-9, you cash ♠ A-K and exit with the ♠ 10. West wins but has to give you a heart trick at the end.

In real life, the USA declarer took the ♡ Q with the king at trick one and led a club at once. East won and returned a heart to take 4NT three down for a score of +300.

That was worth 14 IMPs to Italy whose South was in 3NT after this auction:

West	North	East	South
			1NT
2♣ *	3NT	All Pass	
* Majors			

A heart was led to the queen, ducked, and West ducked the heart return. South now tackled diamonds and had nine easy tricks when the ◇ Q appeared for +600.

Play with the Champions

THE GRAND CANYON

It is Teams; dealer West; Love All. You are South, holding:

♠ Q 9 5 2
♡ K J 10 7 5 3
◇ —
♣ A K 2

The bidding starts:

West	North	East	South
2♠			

East-West are playing Weak Twos.

What does West's 2♠ show?

___

Answer: The Weak Two shows a good six-card suit, Q-10-x-x-x-x or better, and 6-10 HCP. In first or second seat, there will normally be no void, not two singletons, and not four cards in the other major.

West	North	East	South
2♠	Dbl		

What is the nature of North's double?

___

Answer: The double of a Weak Two is played for take-out and shows the same type of hand that would double a 1♠ opening. Expectancy is 12+ HCP, shortage in spades, four hearts and at least three cards in each minor. With a powerful hand, the distributional requirements are not essential.

West	North	East	South
2♠	Dbl	3♠	

How do you take East's raise?

___

Answer: Raising a Weak Two is pre-emptive, especially after a double. Expectancy for East is three-card support and usually 7-11 HCP.

What action should South take over 3♠?

Answer: If West has six spades and East has three, North will be void and you would then have grand slam chances. It would be enough for North to have the spade void, ♡A-Q, and either the ◇A or the ♣Q, for 7♡ to be there.

Can you discover whether partner has the cards needed for the grand slam?

Answer: A bid of 4♡ would be droppable, 5♡ would invite 6♡ but could be passed and a bid of 4♠ would be forcing but would be of no help in discovering whether partner holds the ♡A as well as the other cards needed.

4NT for aces would also not do. If partner shows two aces, you cannot be certain that partner has the red aces. Partner might have a singleton ♠A. You expect the opponents to hold nine spades but relying on that can be risky. There are those who open a Weak Two with a strong five-card suit and some who raise to the three level pre-emptively with a doubleton.

The answer is that you cannot scientifically find out whether partner has the right cards for 7♡. It is hard enough to bid a grand slam when there is no interference. Since it is silly to gamble on a grand slam, you should bid 6♡.

West	North	East	South
2♠	Dbl	3♠	6♡
Pass	6♠		

Now there's a bid you did not expect.

How do you interpret North's 6♠?

Answer: North is intent on a grand slam but is unsure of the best spot. North is asking you to bid a second suit. With hearts only, you bid 7♡, and that's where the auction ends.

West	North	East	South
2♠	Dbl	3♠	6♡
Pass	6♠	Pass	7♡
All Pass			

West leads the ♠ A and this is what you see:

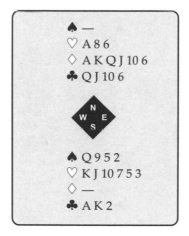

```
            ♠ —
            ♡ A 8 6
            ◇ A K Q J 10 6
            ♣ Q J 10 6

                N
             W     E
                S

            ♠ Q 9 5 2
            ♡ K J 10 7 5 3
            ◇ —
            ♣ A K 2
```

After ruffing the lead, how do you continue?
(While you are considering your play in 7♡, you might also consider
other contracts. How do you play 6♡ after ruffing the lead?
How do you play 7◇ [by North] on a spade lead?)

Answer: In 7♡, the only problem is to avoid a trump loser. What is the normal way to play this holding?

With no other information available, it is slightly superior to play off ♡ A-K rather than the ♡ A followed by the finesse of the ♡ J.

Is there anything here which would make you depart from the normal play?

Answer: When an opponent has pre-empted, the odds favour playing the other opponent to hold the queen of any other suit. A Weak Two is a mild pre-empt. As West has six spades and East three, East is more likely to hold the ♡ Q. Therefore prefer the ♡ A and a heart to the jack.

In 6♡, after ruffing the spade lead, you should lead a low heart from dummy to your jack without cashing the ace first. You can afford to lose a trump but you must be careful to leave a trump in dummy to cater for a spade continuation.

The deal arose in the final of the 1998 International Olympic Grand Prix which resulted in a tie between Brazil and China:

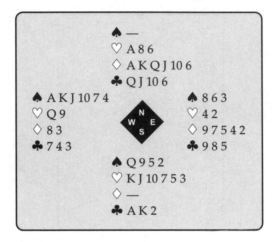

Brazil played in 6♡. South ruffed the spade lead and led the ♡8 to the jack. Twelve tricks, +980.

China played in 7♡ after the auction given. Declarer ruffed the spade lead, cashed the ♡A, and finessed the ♡J. Two down, and 14 IMPs to Brazil.

In 7◇ by North, declarer ruffs the spade lead, draws trumps and cashes the clubs, discovering en route that West began with two diamonds and three clubs. As the spades rate strongly to be 6-3, the hearts must be 2-2. It was a bit much to expect South to bid 7◇ in reply to 6♠.

> Moral: Do not ask partner to do something you can do yourself. If you hold the solid suit, you should insist on making it trumps.

SELF ANALYSIS

It is Teams; dealer North. Game All. You are South, holding:

♠ 9 8 5
♡ A
♢ A 9 7 6 4 3
♣ J 8 6

West	North	East	South
	1♣	1♡	?

What should South do?

Answer: If a 2♢ response is forcing up to the stratosphere, you would pass but if it is merely a one-round force, that is the recommended action even though you have only just enough for a two-over-one response.

West	North	East	South
	1♣	1♡	2♢
2♡	Pass	Pass	?

What should South do now?

Answer: It would be a serious error to pass. When the opponents have bid and raised a suit to the two level, you should almost always compete and try to push them to the three level. This is particularly so if you are short in their suit.

Most of the time they will succeed at the two level, but will be in jeopardy at the three level. It is worth risking a small loss at the three level yourself rather than sell out to 2♡.

A 3♢ rebid puts all your eggs in one basket. That could be foolish if partner has a singleton or is void in diamonds, a distinct possibility.

A 3♣ rebid is better than 3♢ since this allows partner to revert to 3♢ if 3♣ is not attractive, but the best action is a take-out double. This caters for partner holding a 3-4-1-5, a 3-3-1-6, a 4-4-1-4, or more extreme patterns. It is even possible, but unlikely, that partner leaves your double in for penalties. North probably does not hold four spades (as he failed to double 2♡ for take-out).

In real life, South rebid 3♣; North removed to 3◊ which was passed out. West leads the ♡3 to the ♡4, the ♡2 and the ♡A.

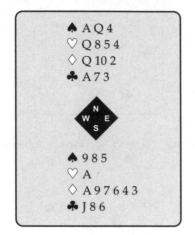

What is the probable heart position?
What problems do you have? What do you play next?

Answer: The hearts are very likely to be 5-3 with East having five headed by K-J or K-10. You have almost certainly two club losers and if the ♠K is wrong, you are in danger of losing two spades, two clubs and hopefully no more than one diamond. There is no virtue in delaying trumps and so you should play the ◊A at trick two followed by another diamond. Both follow low on the first round of trumps and on the next, West wins with the ◊K and East plays the ◊J. West switches to the ♡J.

What do you play from dummy?

Answer: If by some chance West had started with ♡K-J-x, West would not be playing hearts now and so you can assume that East started with ♡K-10-x-x-x. Covering with the ♡Q gains nothing. Playing low may leave you with some endplay possibilities.

You play low from dummy, as does East, and ruff in hand.

What now?

Answer: You need to eliminate the clubs in order to try for some end-position in spades. You should start by ducking a round of clubs. When you lead the ♣6, West plays the ♣4, you duck in dummy, and East wins with the ♣10. As East cannot afford to lead a major suit, East continues with a club, the queen, West following with the ♣2.

How should you proceed from here?

Answer: It would be right to duck this if East started with ♣Q-10 only. As West's ♣4 followed by the ♣2 shows a four-card holding here, there is no benefit in ducking. East will simply play a third club, leaving you to rely on the spade finesse.

Your best move is to win with the ♣A and exit with your third club. This would work particularly well if East began with ♣K-Q-10, and also on the actual deal:

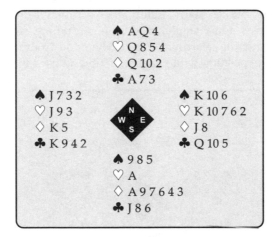

The deal arose in the Vivendi Rosenblum World Open Teams in 1998. Declarer, Bart Bramley of the USA, won East's ♣Q exit with the ace, ruffed a heart and then led the ♣J. West won and switched to the ♠J to the ♠Q and the ♠K. East had a safe exit with the ♡K and declarer had to lose another spade for one down, minus 100. No swing, as 3◇ failed at the other table, too. Had declarer made 3◇, his team would have gained 5 IMPs. The final margin against his team was 105-102.

Had declarer taken ♣Q and exited with a club without ruffing a heart, this would have been the end-position (diagram overleaf):

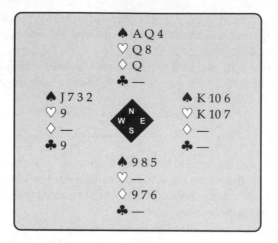

Later Bramley, chastising himself for failing to find the right line, analysed the ending for the World Championship Book. West is on lead and must play a heart. A club gives a ruff-and-discard while a spade exit, covered as cheaply as possible in dummy, would endplay East. South ruffs the heart and plays a diamond to dummy's queen. This is now the position with East still to find a discard:

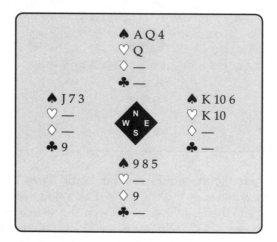

Once West has turned up with the ◇ K and the ♣ K, East must have the ♠ K. If East discards a spade, ♠ A and a low spade drops the king. To retain three spades, East is down to the ♡ K bare. Declarer then exits with the ♡ Q, discarding a spade from hand, and East is endplayed.

West can defeat the contract by switching to a spade when in with the ◇ K. He can later lead another spade on winning with the ♣ K.

NOTHING IS ROTTEN
IN THE STATE OF DENMARK

It is Teams; dealer South; Love All. You are South, holding this hand:

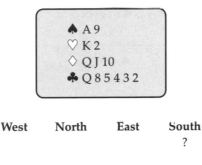

♠ A 9
♡ K 2
◇ Q J 10
♣ Q 8 5 4 3 2

West	North	East	South
			?

What action do you take as dealer?

Answer: The normal opening bid is 1♣. It is somewhat off-beat to open 1NT with a six-card suit in your hand. However, when the deal arose, the bid chosen was 1NT.

West	North	East	South
			1NT
Pass	2◇ *	Pass	2♡
Pass	2NT	Pass	?

* Transfer to hearts

What do you do now?

Answer: Partner's sequence invites game and partner has shown a five-card heart suit. You have only two hearts and so it is not appropriate to support the hearts. With only 12 High Card Points, it would be reasonable to pass, but there is the six-card club suit. You can normally add 1 point for the fifth card in a suit and 1-2 points for the sixth card. Here the clubs are not so strong and so counting just two extra points for length is reasonable. Still, that gives you 14, enough to push to 3NT.

Another potential factor in your favour is that the opponents are unaware of your length in clubs and that might help.

The full auction has been:

West	North	East	South
			1NT
Pass	2◊	Pass	2♡
Pass	2NT	Pass	3NT
All Pass			

West leads the ◊ 3 and this is what you see:

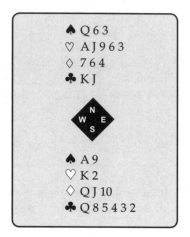

East wins with the ◊ A and returns the ◊ 9 to West's king. You win the third diamond and East discards the ♠ 2.

How many instant tricks do you have?

_____

Answer: You have four tricks on top. The diamond you have won, ♡ A-K, and the ♠ A.

Should you try the hearts for the extra tricks?

_____

Answer: Even if the hearts play for five tricks, that still gives you only seven in all. You cannot make 3NT without some club tricks and therefore you should play on clubs.

What do you need from the clubs?

Answer: A 3-2 break will give you five club tricks, enough to make the contract. In addition, you have to hope that the ♣A is with East, else West will cash two more diamonds on scoring the ♣A.

You play a club to the king and East takes the ace. That hurdle is over. East returns the ♣7 to dummy's jack and West discards the ♠5. Too bad about the club break.

How should you continue?

Answer: You now have one spade, one diamond and two club tricks and so you can make 3NT if you make five tricks in hearts. However, if you cross to the ♡K and play a heart to the jack and it loses, East will play a third club and you cannot escape five losers.

Even if the heart finesse works, you will be in trouble if the hearts are not 3-3. You will have one spade, three hearts, one diamond and two clubs but no chance of nine tricks before they make five.

There is a better plan. What is it?

Answer: You may as well set up the rest of the clubs. That will give you four clubs, two hearts, one spade and one diamond.

How do you proceed?

Answer: You play a heart to the king and cash the ♣Q, followed by another club. East wins and has to play a major suit. A heart return into dummy's A-J will provide the ninth trick.

What if East returns a spade?

Answer: You will have to decide whether to play East for the ♠K and duck the spade for your ninth trick to dummy's ♠Q or take the ♠A, cash the clubs and hope that the heart finesse works.

If West has the ♠K and the ♡Q, the clubs will squeeze West in the majors. In addition, if West has the ♠K, you can reduce West to the ♠K and one heart (a 'show-up' squeeze) after trick eleven.

If a low spade comes back, which play will you adopt?

Answer: On a spade return it is certainly attractive to rise with the ace and rattle off the clubs. You would be a hero if the complete hand looked like this:

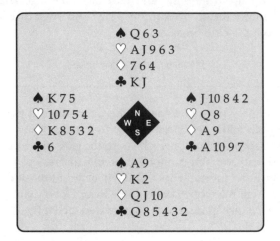

♠ Q 6 3
♡ A J 9 6 3
◇ 7 6 4
♣ K J

♠ K 7 5
♡ 10 7 5 4
◇ K 8 5 3 2
♣ 6

♠ J 10 8 4 2
♡ Q 8
◇ A 9
♣ A 10 9 7

♠ A 9
♡ K 2
◇ Q J 10
♣ Q 8 5 4 3 2

This will be the end-position:

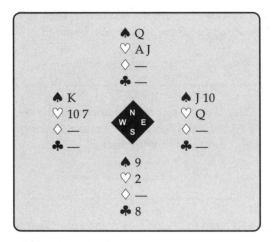

♠ Q
♡ A J
◇ —
♣ —

♠ K
♡ 10 7
◇ —
♣ —

♠ J 10
♡ Q
◇ —
♣ —

♠ 9
♡ 2
◇ —
♣ 8

When the last club is played, West has to let go a heart in order to retain the ♠ K. You now lead a heart, and rise with the ace to the deafening applause of the crowd as the ♡ Q falls offside.

This is a pretty scenario but when East returns the low spade you should duck it to dummy's queen, since the ♠K is almost certainly with East.

Why?

Answer: If East lacked the ♠K, East would have switched to a spade after taking the ♣A to try to hit partner's entry. East would not have played a club back at that point.

There is good news and there is more good news. If you duck the spade exit, dummy's ♠Q wins – and if you rise with the ♠A and rely on the heart finesse, that works too.

The deal arose in the 1992 World Open Teams Olympiad round-robin match between Denmark and Mauritius. Lars Blakset of Denmark made 3NT via the play described (with the auction as given) to gain 8 IMPs.

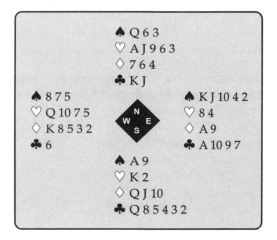

```
              ♠ Q 6 3
              ♡ A J 9 6 3
              ◇ 7 6 4
              ♣ K J
♠ 8 7 5                    ♠ K J 10 4 2
♡ Q 10 7 5      N          ♡ 8 4
◇ K 8 5 3 2   W   E        ◇ A 9
♣ 6             S          ♣ A 10 9 7
              ♠ A 9
              ♡ K 2
              ◇ Q J 10
              ♣ Q 8 5 4 3 2
```

At the other table the Danish East-West stole the contract in 3♠, one down, for minus 50.

BROWNED OFF

It is Teams; dealer West; E/W Vulnerable. You are South, holding:

```
♠ A Q 9 2
♡ K 9 6 5 4 2
◇ A
♣ A 2
```

The bidding starts:

West	North	East	South
1◇	Pass	Pass	?

What do you do?

Answer: You have a strong hand and both majors. It would be an error to bid any number of hearts since there may be a better spot in spades. You should double (for take-out).

West	North	East	South
1◇	Pass	Pass	Dbl
2♣	Pass	2◇	?

What now?

Answer: There are two basic choices: you can double again, still for take-out of course, or you can bid hearts. To bid hearts would suggest a one-suited hand and so double is still best as it brings both majors into play.

At the table, South chose to bid hearts.

If so, how many hearts should you bid?

Answer: A sound way to judge doubler's rebid is to count losers. You have four losers: one in spades, two in hearts and one in clubs. Having four losers indicates that you have nine playing tricks and so a jump to 3♡ is suitable.

In real life, the auction went:

West	North	East	South
1◇	Pass	Pass	Dbl
2♣	Pass	2◇	4♡
All Pass			

Had South jumped to 3♡, North has enough to raise to 4♡.

West leads the ◇ K and this is what you see:

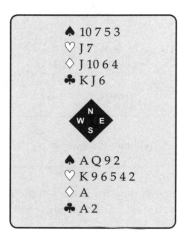

East plays the ◇ 5 and you win with the ace.

How do you continue?

Answer: As West can have at most 7 points in the minors, West will have strength in the majors. As West bid both minors, the major-suit honours will be short, perhaps ♡ A-Q and ♠ K-x.

Continue with a low heart from hand.

West wins with the ♡ A and switches to the ♣ 4.

You play low from dummy, East inserts the ♣ 9, and you win with the ♣ A.

What do you make of the heart position?

Answer: Apparently West started with the ♡A singleton and that means East still has ♡Q-10-8.

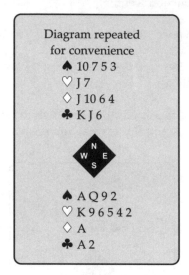

Diagram repeated
for convenience
♠ 10 7 5 3
♡ J 7
◇ J 10 6 4
♣ K J 6

N
W E
S

♠ A Q 9 2
♡ K 9 6 5 4 2
◇ A
♣ A 2

What do you play next?

Answer: It is time to test the spades. You cash the ♠A, West playing the ♠J, and continue with the ♠Q, West winning with the ♠K.

What is the spade position?

Answer: West began with ♠K-J doubleton and East with three low spades.

What do you know about the hand patterns of East and West?

Answer: As West began with only two spades and one heart, West will hold ten cards in the minors. As West bid diamonds and clubs, West might hold 5-5 in the minors, or six diamonds and four clubs. If West were 6-4, East would be 2-4 and would have chosen clubs. As East gave preference to diamonds, you can place East with three diamonds. That means West began with a 2-1-5-5 pattern and East with a 3-4-3-3.

West exits with a club and you play the ♣J from dummy which wins.

What next?

Answer: You have lost two tricks already and East's ♡ Q-10-8 threatens to score two more tricks for the defence. If you lead the ♡ J, East covers with the queen and still has ♡ 10-8. As you have no more trumps in dummy after the jack, you might well lose two trump tricks to East later.

How do you propose to deal with the problem of East's trumps?

Answer: The essential strategy when you cannot pick up an opponent's trump holding by finessing is to reduce your trump holding to the same number of trumps as your opponent.

As you have two trumps more than East you must organise two ruffs in your hand. After winning with the ♣ J, you ruff a diamond. A spade to dummy's ten takes you back to dummy.

What do you play next?

Answer: This was the complete deal:

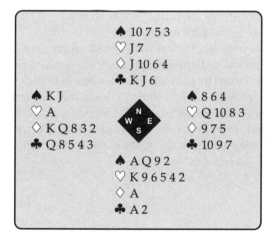

After the play so far, these are the cards that remain (diagram overleaf):

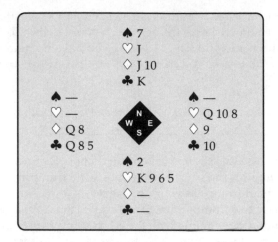

There are two paths to success from here.

Line A is to cash the ♣ K, discarding your last spade, and ruff another diamond. This leaves you with just K-9-6 in hearts. You exit with a low heart to the jack and queen, and East has to lead a trump from ♡ 10-8, giving you the last two tricks and the contract.

The successful declarer was Terry Brown, who won the Brilliancy Prize (shared) for his play on this deal from the 1999 Australian National Open Teams Championship.

Brown chose to finish East off with Line B: in the above diagrammed position, he ruffed a diamond and then led a heart to the jack and queen. A heart return by East would allow South to pick up the trumps and so East played a club, but it made no difference. Declarer discarded the spade and won with dummy's king. Either card from dummy would now force East to ruff ahead of declarer, who would over-ruff as cheaply as possible and nullify East's trump holding.

Rather well played, don't you agree?

JUNIOR HIGH

It is Pairs; dealer West; Love All. You, South, hold:

```
♠ A Q 10 9 8 2
♡ Q 7
♢ Q J
♣ A 8 5
```

The bidding starts:

West	North	East	South
Pass	Pass	1♡*	?
* Five-card majors			

What should South do?

Answer: You have 15 HCP but the red-suit honours are of doubtful value. If you played intermediate jump-overcalls (11-15 points and a decent six-plus suit), you would jump to 2♠. Playing other methods, it is enough to overcall with 1♠. The hand is not strong enough to double first and bid spades later (as that would show a five-loser hand).

West	North	East	South
Pass	Pass	1♡	1♠
2♠¹	Dbl²	3♡	?
¹ Heart support, strong, inviting game			
² Spade support but not enough to bid 3♠			

What should South do now?

Answer: Partner will have three spades for you and that gives you a total of nine trumps.

The Law of Total Tricks recommends that you bid to the same

---

number of tricks as you have trumps. That means you should bid for nine tricks. Bid 3♠.

West	North	East	South
Pass	Pass	1♡	1♠
2♠	Dbl	3♡	3♠
4♡	Pass	Pass	?

And now what?

Answer: West is a passed hand, East has opened third in hand, West has made a strong game invitation and East has rejected it. If these opponents are on the level, 4♡ is not going to make. You should double and take what you can from 4♡ doubled.

In the event, South bid 4♠ and West doubled. The contract became 4♠ doubled and West leads the ♡3. This is what you see:

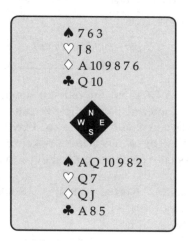

♠ 7 6 3
♡ J 8
♢ A 10 9 8 7 6
♣ Q 10

♠ A Q 10 9 8 2
♡ Q 7
♢ Q J
♣ A 8 5

East wins with the ♡A and returns the ♡9 to West's king. At trick three, West switches to the ♢K.

What do you make of the heart position?

Answer: East figures to have started with five hearts headed by the ace and West with four to the king. It is possible, but less likely, that East began with four hearts and West with five. Those who play five-card majors do often open in third seat with a strong four-card suit but A-x-x-x hardly qualifies as 'strong'.

How do you estimate the high-card values held by East and West?

Answer: You and dummy have 22 HCP between you. That leaves 18 for East-West. As West has made a strong game invitation, you can be very confident that East has opened light. So far you have seen the ♡ K and the ◇ K from West, but West figures to have 3-4 more points. If West began with 9 HCP, then East also had 9 initially. If West started with 10 HCP, then East started with only 8. No wonder East tried to sign off in 3♡.

After East's 3♡ sign-off, West's 4♡ was a breach of discipline.

What might justify that?

Answer: West is bound to have a short suit somewhere. With a 2-4-3-4 or even a 2-4-2-5 pattern, West could not afford to bid 4♡.

Where will the singleton be?

Answer: Clearly in spades or in diamonds. As West could not expect to score two tricks from the hearts, West might well have led the ◇ K if that was the singleton. The 4♡ bid is more likely to be based on a singleton in the most useful spot, the enemy suit. You can reasonably expect West to be singleton or void in spades.

You take the ◇ A and lead the ♠ 3; East follows with the ♠ 4.

What is the normal play with this trump combination?

Answer: In the absence of any knowledge of the opponents' cards, you should finesse the queen. This brings in the suit for no loser if West has J-x or jack singleton (assuming you can return to dummy to repeat the finesse).

Assuming that West has a singleton spade, if it is the jack, playing the queen will work. If it is the king, then you need to play the ace. If West has a low singleton, then you need to play the ♠ 8, the ♠ 9 or the ♠ 10 from hand.

There is an element of guesswork here and in practice declarer finessed the ten which held the trick, West playing the ♠ 5.

What do you know now?

___

Answer: East began with ♠ K-J-4 and still has ♠ K-J. You need to return to dummy to repeat the finesse. You can return to dummy via a successful guess in clubs or by ruffing the third round of clubs.

Does it matter if you misguess the clubs?

___

Answer: Absolutely. Picking up the clubs is vital.

What do you know about the West hand?

___

Answer: West is known to have a singleton spade and presumed to hold four hearts. The play of the ◇ K looks as though it is from king-doubleton. (If West started with one spade and one diamond, and so a 1-4-1-7 pattern, you have no hope of reaching dummy for a second spade finesse). If West has two diamonds, that leaves West with six clubs, and therefore East began with two clubs. You cannot reach dummy with a third-round club ruff, as East will over-ruff.

You lead a low club and West plays low.

Which club do you play from dummy?

___

Answer: East has turned up with the ♡ A and ♠ K-J, West with the ♡ K and the ◇ K. If East has the ♣ K, that would give West the ♣ J and 7 HCP at most, hardly enough to make a strong game invitation, let alone that 4♡ bid. You should play West for the ♣ K.

You rise with dummy's ♣ Q, which wins and repeat the spade finesse. You cash the ♣ A and ruff the third club in dummy, but sure enough East over-ruffs. Still, you have made your doubled game and gained a top score. This was the full deal:

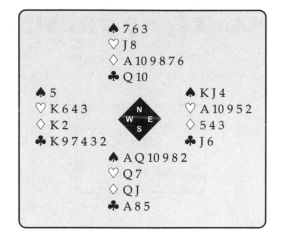

The bidding and play went as described in the 1998 Junior Pairs Championship in Lille. East-West were the eventual winners, Tomasz Przyjemski and Marcin Zaremba (who did well to bid 4♡ which would be only one down and a good save against the North-South part-score in spades). The successful declarer was Rafal Rokoszewski of Poland.

Could the defence have done better?

Answer: Not really, except as speculation. East could have played the ♠J on the first round of spades. Upon winning with the queen, perhaps South would have played East for ♠K-J doubleton and laid down the ♠A. As against that, by playing low East gave South a good chance to get the spades wrong. South may still have played West for a singleton spade on the bidding.

What about declarer's play? Any comment?

Answer: As declarer finessed the ♠10 on the first round of spades, why did he not lead the ♠7 or the ♠6 from dummy and run it? It is true that East might then have covered with the jack but that could easily have been an error (if West had, say, the ♠Q singleton). My guess is that declarer was planning to finesse the ♠Q and so led low from dummy. When East followed low, declarer thought some more about the bidding and the probable spade layout.

Such thinking was well-rewarded.

NO NAMES, NO TRUMPETS

It is Teams; dealer South; E/W Vulnerable. You are North, holding:

♠ Q J 9 7
♡ 10 5 4
◇ K
♣ K 8 7 4 2

The bidding starts:

West	North	East	South
			1NT*
Pass	?		
* 12-14			

What action would you take?

Answer: You have the majority of points and so you are more likely to take seven tricks than the opponents, but the shape is not attractive for 1NT. If partner has a four-card major, that is likely to be safer than 1NT (even a 4-3 heart fit is likely to play better than 1NT) and Stayman would locate a major.

The reality, of course, is that partner need not have a major and with only five clubs you do not want to sail as high as 3♣ and perhaps hit partner with a doubleton.

Despite your misgivings, your strength might protect you and you should pass. The auction continues:

West	North	East	South
			1NT
Pass	Pass	Dbl*	Pass
Pass	?		

* Hearts and a minor, or very strong

What action should North take now?

Answer: At pairs you could gamble on a pass but teams is no place for heroics. As East is likely to have hearts plus a minor, you can be confident which minor East holds. Remove the double to 2♣. If you have some method to show a one-suiter or a two-suiter, use that but do not stick around to see whether blood will flow. It may well be yours.

At the table North passed 1NT doubled.

Now move to the South seat and try your hand at playing this. West leads the ◊Q:

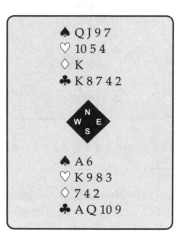

♠ Q J 9 7
♡ 10 5 4
◊ K
♣ K 8 7 4 2

♠ A 6
♡ K 9 8 3
◊ 7 4 2
♣ A Q 10 9

East takes the ◊K with the ace and returns the ◊9, which holds. The ◊5 comes next, West winning with the ◊10 (you have pitched two hearts from dummy). West switches to the ♡6: East wins with the ♡A and continues with the ♡2, won by your king, the ♡J from West.

What do you do now?

Answer: If you can score five club tricks, you will have made your contract. If the clubs are 2-2 you can easily score five club tricks via the ♣A, the ♣Q, the ♣10 and overtaking the ♣9. If the clubs are 3-1, there is a problem.

What is it?

Answer: A singleton jack is no worry but if either opponent has ♣J-x-x, then the clubs will be blocked and you will have to win the fourth round in your hand. That will leave you one trick short.

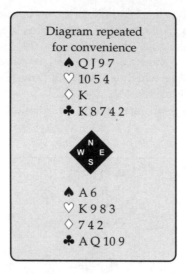

Diagram repeated
for convenience
♠ Q J 9 7
♡ 10 5 4
◇ K
♣ K 8 7 4 2

N
W E
S

♠ A 6
♡ K 9 8 3
◇ 7 4 2
♣ A Q 10 9

What do you make of the red suits?

Answer: As West has no certain quick entry, West would have cashed the diamond tricks with long diamonds. Therefore West did not start with five diamonds. As West led the ◇ Q, and later played a low diamond and the ◇ 10, West still has the ◇ J and the diamonds are blocked.

This means that East started with four hearts (to the A-Q on the play so far) and five diamonds. That gives East nine red cards to West's six, and so clubs may well be three with West and one with East.

How should you play the clubs?

Answer: If West started with ♣ J-x-x, you could try the effect of the ♣ 9, hoping to sneak it past West. The trouble is that this relies on an opponent's error (West could cover the ♣ 9 to block the suit) and would look more than a little foolish if East won with the ♣ J singleton or with the ♣ J doubleton.

You may as well play clubs from the top and hope for a 2-2 break. Everyone follows on the ♣ A, but East shows out on the ♣ Q.

What do you do now?

Answer: Your best hope now is that East has the ♠K. You cross to dummy with the third club and lead the ♠Q. If that holds, you will be able to make two spades, one heart and four clubs.

East plays low on the ♠Q, so do you, and West takes the king. These are the cards you have left:

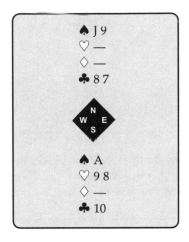

West cashes ◊J. You need the rest of the tricks.

What do you discard from dummy and from hand?

Answer: With the ♠K also with West, it is now certain that East's double was based not on strength but on hearts and diamonds. West has already shown up with two hearts and will have no more, and this will be West's last diamond (else there is no hope). That leaves West with only spades left.

Once you come to that decision, the solution is simple. Discard the ♠9 from dummy and the ♠A from your hand. West's spade lead will be taken with dummy's jack and on this you will discard your ♣10, finally being able to unblock. Having made 1NT doubled you can then have a word to partner about leaving 1NT doubled in.

The full deal is shown overleaf:

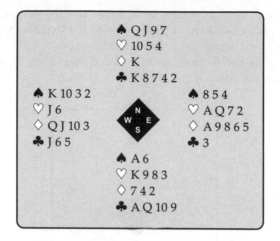

After three rounds of diamonds, West blocking the suit, heart to the ace, heart to the king, three rounds of clubs and the losing spade finesse, these were the last four cards:

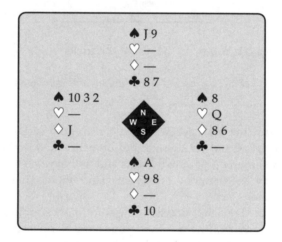

When West cashed the ◇ J, South threw a club from both hands. Now South had to win the spade exit and concede the last two tricks to East. That was two down, for minus 300.

Obviously South could no longer complain about North's bidding when the contract was there with four cards to go.

The deal arose in the semi-finals of the 1992 Olympiad Women's Teams between Germany and Great Britain. No names will be mentioned here, but suffice to say that none of the four players would want this deal on their C.V.

A TOUCH OF BRILLIANCE

It is Teams; dealer West; E/W Vulnerable. You are South, holding:

```
♠ K Q 9 8 7
♡ —
♢ J 9 7 6 5
♣ K Q 3
```

The bidding starts:

West	North	East	South
Pass	Pass	1♡	?

What should South do?

Answer: The options are 1♠, double and 2♡ (Michaels Cue-bid). The least attractive is double: with five cards in the other major and a strong suit, it is better to show the five-card holding, enabling partner to support with three. If you double and partner bids clubs, you will have a niggling doubt that partner might hold three spades, but to double first and bid spades later shows a stronger hand than this in terms of high cards.

The Michaels Cue-bid, 2♡, is certainly reasonable as it shows five spades as well as a five-card minor. The drawback is that the right spot could be in clubs but it will be very difficult to find that strain if you show a spade-diamond two-suiter. Choose the 1♠ overall.

West	North	East	South
Pass	Pass	1♡	1♠
2♡	3♠ *	4♡	?

* Constructive

What now?

Answer: Bid 4♠. You might make it and if not, it could easily be a very cheap sacrifice.

The bidding continues:

West	North	East	South
Pass	Pass	1♡	1♠
2♡	3♠	4♡	4♠
Pass	Pass	5♡	?

And now what?

Answer: There are two sound reasons for passing. You have pushed the vulnerable opponents to the five-level where they might be in some jeopardy. Further, you do not know partner's values in hearts. If partner has some defensive potential in hearts, defending will be the better choice. If partner has nothing of value in hearts, it may be right to sacrifice in 5♠.

In such cases, the player with the shortage in the opponents' suit should not bid on in the direct seat, but should pass the decision to partner. If partner has values in hearts, partner can choose to defend by passing or even doubling 5♡. If partner has no heart strength, he can still choose to defend but might also choose 5♠, particularly at this vulnerability.

West	North	East	South
Pass	Pass	1♡	1♠
2♡	3♠	4♡	4♠
Pass	Pass	5♡	Pass
Pass	5♠	Dbl	All Pass

West leads the ♡7 and you can see that partner has made a sound choice in bidding 5♠ (diagram on next page). If either opponent has a singleton spade or a singleton club, 5♡ would be unbeatable.

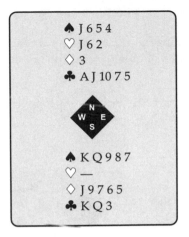

♠ J 6 5 4
♡ J 6 2
◇ 3
♣ A J 10 7 5

N
W E
S

♠ K Q 9 8 7
♡ —
◇ J 9 7 6 5
♣ K Q 3

East plays the ♡K; you ruff. When you play the ♠K, all follow low.

What is happening in spades?

_____

Answer: The spades are almost certainly 3-1 and an opponent is planning to win the next spade and play a third round so as to reduce dummy's ruffing potential.

How do you continue?

_____

Answer: You have only two top losers, one in spades and one in diamonds. If the opponents are planning to stop you ruffing diamonds in dummy, you can counter by ruffing hearts in your hand. If you can ruff all of dummy's hearts, you might actually make this contract.

Where are your entries to dummy for the ruffs in hearts?

_____

Answer: There are two entries in clubs, one of which requires that you overtake one of your honours with dummy's ace. You play the ♣Q to dummy's ace, ruff a heart, lead the ♣3 to dummy's ten (both follow) and ruff dummy's last heart.

What next?

Answer: It is time to draw trumps and so you lead the ♠Q from hand.

The late Dick Cummings won the prize for the best-played hand in the 1975 Australian National Open Teams for his skillful display on this deal:

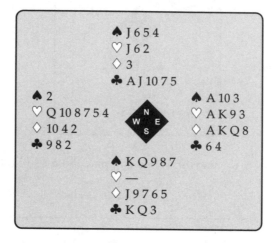

East won the ♠Q exit and continued with a top diamond followed by another diamond, ruffed in dummy. Now the ♠J drew the last trump as declarer discarded the blocking ♣K. The last three tricks were won by dummy's clubs.

As you can see, 5♡ is unbeatable with just two losers in clubs. With only nineteen trumps for the two sides but twenty-two tricks made, it poses an interesting exercise for those who follow the Law of Total Tricks. The double fit in the black suits helps explain the anomaly.

East might have tried to defeat the contract.

How?

Answer: In with the ♠A, East might have led the ◊8, hoping to reach West's hand for a club ruff in return. Declarer would play the ◊J, a cost-nothing move, which would lead to 5♠ doubled making with an overtrick.

THUD AND BLUNDER

It is Teams; dealer North; E/W Vulnerable. West holds:

♠ J 4 3
♡ A J 10 9 6 3
♢ Q J
♣ 6 4

The bidding goes:

West	North	East	South
	Pass	Pass	1♣ [1]
1♡	2♢ [2]	2♠	3NT
All Pass			

[1] Artificial, strong (16+ points)
[2] Natural, 4–7 points

What should West lead?

Answer: When the choice is between leading your own suit and leading partner's suit, you should choose your own suit when you have a good sequence and outside entries, otherwise prefer partner's suit, particularly when you have length there. Lead the ♠ 3.

In practice, the lead was the ♡ J and this is what you see (diagram on next page):

Dummy
♠ 9 5 2
♡ 7 5
♢ A 10 8 7 5 2
♣ 9 2

You
♠ J 4 3
♡ A J 10 9 6 3
♢ Q J
♣ 6 4

Trick one goes: ♡ J – ♡ 5 – ♡ K – ♡ 2. East switches to the ♠ 10.

What do you make of that?

Answer: Clearly partner began with the singleton ♡ K, else a heart return would have finished declarer off.

What follows from that?

Answer: South began with ♡ Q-x-x-x. File that away for future reference.

What can you deduce from the fact that East has switched to the ♠ 10?

Answer: Because the ♠ 9 is in dummy, the ♠ 10 switch means that East has a 'surround' position over dummy, either ♠ Q-10-8-x(-x) or ♠ K-10-8-x(-x).

South wins the ♠ 10 switch with the queen and so you can place East with spades originally headed by K-10-8. South continues with the ♣ A and the ♣ K, East following with the ♣ 10 and the ♣ J, and then plays the ♣ 3 . . .

What do you discard on that?

Answer: Since your hearts are not useful other than preventing declarer from making a trick with the queen, you can comfortably afford a heart discard.

East wins with the ♣ Q and continues with the ♠ 6. Declarer wins with the ♠ A and plays off three more rounds of clubs.

What are your three discards?

Answer: On the basis that your reading of the spade position is correct, you should let hearts go, so that your last four cards are the ♠ J, the ♡ A and ◇ Q-J. This ensures declarer is one off on the actual deal:

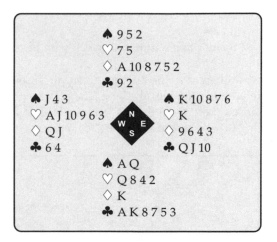

The four-card ending will be something like:

If you ever needed evidence that you can improve your results significantly by focusing on defensive technique, this deal is it. In the

1998 World Championships, three declarers played in 3NT and they all made it, thanks to indifferent defence by West. At one table in the final of the McConnell Cup (Women's Teams), this was the auction with Germany North-South:

West	North	East	South
Fischer	von Arnim	Weigkricht	Auken
	Pass	Pass	1♣
2◊ *	Pass	2♡	3♣
Pass	3◊	Pass	3NT
All Pass			

* Spades and a minor, or weak with hearts

The bidding was different to the auction given earlier but that should not have mattered other than for the lead. The play went as described, but West discarded the ◊ Q on the last club instead of a heart. In the four-card ending (as above, but with the ♡ 10 replacing the ◊ Q):

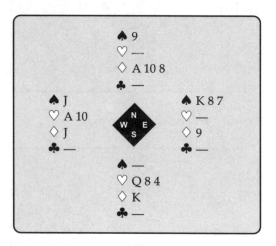

Declarer could now play the ◊ K and overtake with dummy's ◊ A to score two more diamonds for +430.

At the other table of the final,, with Austria North-South:

West	North	East	South
Stawowy	Terraneo	Farwig	Erhart
	Pass	Pass	1♣
1♡	Pass	Pass	Dbl
Pass	3◊	Pass	3NT
All Pass			

Without any inkling that partner had spades, West here too naturally led a heart, taken by the king. As South had not revealed significant length in clubs, East opted to switch to the ♣Q. When declarer ducked, East played another club. South won and ran the rest of the clubs. West discarded three hearts and one spade, and so came down to only two hearts. Declarer led a heart, won the spade return and the next heart forced the ace and set up her ♡Q for nine tricks, +400, and 1 IMP to Germany.

As the play had gone, with declarer not yet scoring two spade tricks, West needed to hold on to three hearts and two diamonds, coming down to the ♠J, ♡A-10-9, ◊Q-J.

This would have been the six-card ending:

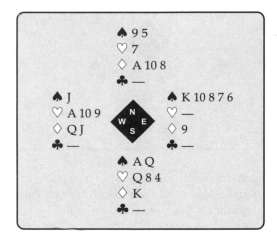

Having lost two tricks, no matter how she wriggles, declarer cannot come to more than three more tricks as long as the defence does not slip. If declarer here exits with a low heart, West wins cheaply and must switch to a diamond. If West errs and switches to the ♠J, South wins and cashes the ♠A. This squeezes West in the red suits. If West lets go a diamond, dummy's diamonds come good after declarer overtakes the ◊K. If West lets go a heart, coming down to the ♡A bare, declarer plays a heart to set up the ♡Q with the ◊K as the entry.

The reader might think these errors were considerable in a world championship final, but they pale in comparison with those committed by West in the Rosenblum (Open Teams) semi-final between Brazil and Sweden. The bidding went as given and despite East's spade bid, the lead was a heart to the king (note how a spade lead would have made life much easier for the defence). East switched to the ♠10, taken by the queen. South now played the ♣A, the ♣K and a third club. On this

West discarded a spade – not a clever move as it completely cut out East's spades. As there was no longer any point in continuing spades, East switched to a diamond to remove pressure on partner on the forthcoming run of the clubs. The Brazilian declarer, Gabriel Chagas, won with the ◊ K and cashed three more clubs, West discarding his other diamond and two hearts.

This was the position:

```
                    ♠ 9
                    ♡ 7
                    ◊ A 10
                    ♣ —
   ♠ J                          ♠ K 8 7 6
   ♡ A J 9         N            ♡ —
   ◊ —          W     E         ◊ —
   ♣ —             S            ♣ —
                    ♠ A
                    ♡ Q 8 4
                    ◊ —
                    ♣ —
```

Demonstrating that he knew full well what was going on, Chagas now cashed the ♠ A and exited with a low heart, forcing West to concede a heart trick to declarer for the ninth trick and +400.

With the heart position clear-cut, a blunder of the magnitude of the spade discard on the third club is scarcely credible at this expert level. Just remember that everyone is fallible the next time your partner falls from grace.

COUNTDOWN

It is Teams; N/S Vulnerable. You are South, the dealer, holding:

```
♠ A J 6
♡ 5 4
◇ A K 2
♣ A K 10 9 2
```

The bidding starts:

West	North	East	South
			2NT
Pass	3◇ *	Pass	3♡
Pass	4NT	Pass	?
	* Transfer to hearts		

What does 4NT mean?

Answer: It would be sensible to treat 4NT here as an invitation to slam including five hearts. It also makes sense to use 4NT as asking for aces or as asking for key cards with hearts set as trumps. The answer is not a matter of right or wrong but simply what agreements you have with partner. Clearly it is important for you both to have the same agreement here. Passing Blackwood is frowned upon in the best circles – and most others as well.

Suppose your agreement is that 4NT is Roman Key-Card Blackwood with hearts as trumps. The auction proceeds:

West	North	East	South
			2NT
Pass	3◇	Pass	3♡
Pass	4NT	Pass	5♣
Pass	7NT	All Pass	

Your 5♣ showed 0 or 3 key cards, clearly three for the 2NT opening. You await the appearance of dummy with keen interest. The lead is the ♠ 8 and this is what you see (diagram overleaf):

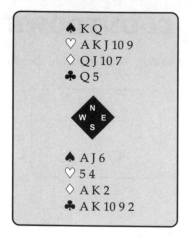

♠ K Q
♡ A K J 10 9
◇ Q J 10 7
♣ Q 5

N
W E
S

♠ A J 6
♡ 5 4
◇ A K 2
♣ A K 10 9 2

Well, you can see why partner was excited!

How many tricks can you count?

Answer: You have twelve tricks on top.

Where is the thirteenth?

Answer: Either from the ♣J coming down within three rounds (that is a bit above 50%), otherwise from the hearts.

How do you proceed?

Answer: As you will one heart finesse at most, you may as well start by cashing the ♡A. If the queen happens to drop (don't hold your breath), the hand is over rather quickly. Nope, no ♡Q appears.

What next?

Answer: Your clubs have never been mentioned and so an opponent may discard one to their later regret. To force one or both opponents to discard, you should cash your diamonds next.

What will you discard on the fourth diamond?

Answer: You need only one extra trick from the clubs and so you can afford to throw a club. That may also convince an opponent that it is safe to throw a club.

When you cash the diamonds, West follows to four rounds, East discards one heart and one spade.

What now?

Answer: It is time to test the clubs. You must try clubs before hearts since if the ♣ J comes down, you need not risk the hearts.

Should you finesse on the second round of clubs?

Answer: That might work but West might have ♣ J-x or ♣ J-x-x. If so, you have gone down when you might have made easily. The odds definitely favour playing the clubs from the top.

You cash the ♣ Q, the ♣ A, the ♣ K and it turns out that East began with ♣ J-x-x-x. Curses, the club finesse would have worked.

What do you know so far?

Answer: West began with four diamonds and two clubs, and East began with two diamonds and four clubs. The position you now see is (diagram overleaf):

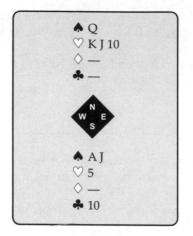

How do you proceed?

Answer: You cash the ♠ A and the ♠ J next and see what happens. East follows to the ace but discards a heart on the ♠ J.

What do you make of that?

Answer: East followed to the first spade, threw a spade on the diamonds and followed to only one more spade; West therefore began with five spades. Now you know the whole picture: West started with a 5-2-4-2 pattern and East with a 3-4-2-4. In order to hold on to the ♣ J, East has had to throw two hearts. You therefore play the hearts from the top, knowing that the queen must now drop.

That is precisely how Charlotte Koch Palmund played the hand to make 7NT and gain 13 IMPs for Denmark against Italy who stopped in 6NT. The story would have been excellent if East had started with ♡ Q-x-x-x, but it in no way detracts from Koch Palmund's fine play that West began with ♡ Q-x all along.

WITHOUT VISIBLE MEANS OF SUPPORT

It is Teams; dealer: West; N/S Vulnerable. You, South, hold:

♠ A Q J 8 6 4
♡ 8 7 5 3
◇ Q 6 2
♣ —

The bidding starts:

West	North	East	South
1♣	1◇	Pass	?

What action would you take as South?

Answer: A 1♠ response would be fine if forcing. If not, then your best first move is 2♣, the Unassuming Cue-bid, to show a strong raise. If partner jumps to 5◇, your hand will not be a disappointment. After a less exuberant rebid you will be able to introduce your spades. If partner shows moderate values with a rebid of 2◇, you can now show the spades and this will be a one-round force.

West	North	East	South
1♣	1◇	Pass	2♣
Pass	3♣	Pass	?

What do you make of the 3♣ bid?

Answer: The return cue-bid shows a powerful overcall and is forcing to game. It denies a second suit (partner would bid 2♡ or 2♠ with a four-card major and a good hand) and expects you to bid 3NT with a stopper in clubs.

What do you do now?

Answer: You cannot keep those spades hidden forever and so you bid 3♠.

What does that show?

Answer: Since partner has denied a four-card major, the expectancy for 3♠ is a five-card suit and partner should raise with three. 3♠ cannot be passed, as partner's 3♣ committed the partnership to game.

West	North	East	South
1♣	1◇	Pass	2♣
Pass	3♣	Pass	3♠
Pass	3NT	Pass	?

What do you make of 3NT?

Answer: Either partner has only one stopper in clubs and was hoping for help there from you, or partner has the clubs well held but had concerns about the spades for 3NT and has now been reassured by 3♠.

What do you do now?

Answer: If partner has only one stopper in clubs, then 3NT is unlikely to fare well. If partner's concern was the spade suit, then a doubleton opposite will be adequate support for your suit. 4♠ might even be playable opposite a singleton. Given your lack of entries outside spades, your spade suit may be of little value in no-trumps if partner is short in spades.

You may as well rebid the spades. This will show a strong six-card, or longer, suit and if partner does not like that, partner can always revert to diamonds.

The full auction:

West	North	East	South
1♣	1◇	Pass	2♣
Pass	3♣	Pass	3♠
Pass	3NT	Pass	4♠
All Pass			

The lead is the ♣ A and this is what you see:

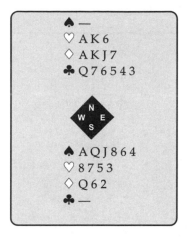

♠ —
♡ A K 6
♢ A K J 7
♣ Q 7 6 5 4 3

N
W E
S

♠ A Q J 8 6 4
♡ 8 7 5 3
♢ Q 6 2
♣ —

Hmmm. A doubleton opposite would have been welcome and a singleton tolerable, but a void is not the stuff dreams are made of.

Still, you can (as always) see partner's problem. Having overcalled on a powerful four-card suit, North would not want to bid 5♢ .

You ruff the ♣ A lead. What next?

Answer: You have 26 points between you and dummy. That leaves 14 for the opposition. The ♣ K is almost certainly with West and that should give protection against being forced.

You can play off three rounds of trumps, conceding a trick to the king *en route*. If spades are 4-3 as normal, you will have to concede a second spade trick, but you will still be able to score four spade tricks, four diamonds and two hearts.

You cash the ♠ A, all following, and then play the ♠ Q. West wins with the king, East following, and switches to the ♡ Q. Dummy wins and you ruff a club to hand to cash the ♠ J. If all follow to this, you can simply play off the diamonds and let the defender with the remaining trump ruff at will. You will still have a trump left and will then make five spades, two hearts and three diamonds.

When you cash the ♠ J, West shows out.

Now what?

Answer: Play on diamonds. When they survive for three rounds, ruff a club and play a heart. You have made five spades and five red suit winners. The full deal was:

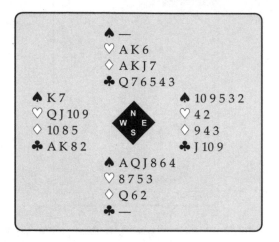

In the 1979 Bermuda Bowl final, Dano De Falco of Italy made 4♠ as described after the auction as given. That was worth 10 IMPs to Italy as Bobby Goldman of the USA made ten tricks in 3♠ at the other table, after the bidding:

West	North	East	South
1♡	2♣	Pass	2♠
Pass	3◊	Pass	3♠
All Pass			

In spite of this board, USA won the final by 253-248 IMPs.

South might well have started trumps by playing ace and then a low one. This gains if either opponent has K-x as you then will not need to rely on diamonds 3-3. If East wins the second spade cheaply and leads a club, South needs to ruff. If South discards a heart instead and West began with ♠ K-10-x-x and five clubs, West could win with the top club and play a third club. If East can ruff this with ♠9, uppercutting declarer, there will be two more trumps to lose. As the bidding almost certainly marks West with the ♠ K, playing the ♠ A and then a low one will not damage you if trumps are 4-3.